IT'S YOUR STORY TO TELL

Sharon,

Thank you for all
the support!

-Maron

IT'S YOUR STORY TO TELL

ESSAYS ON IDENTITY FROM
A MESSY LIFE WELL LIVED

MARYANN LOMBARDI

NEW DEGREE PRESS

COPYRIGHT © 2021 MARYANN LOMBARDI

All rights reserved.

IT'S YOUR STORY TO TELL

ESSAYS ON IDENTITY FROM A MESSY LIFE WELL LIVED

ISBN   978-1-63730-802-8 *Paperback*
           978-1-63730-861-5 *Kindle Ebook*
           978-1-63730-986-5 *Ebook*

To the coolest kid on the planet, who will probably never read this book because they are a teenager, and teenagers usually think the stuff their parents do is whack anyway.

To Luciana, who would have absolutely read it if she were still with us.

"Writing gives you the illusion of control, and then you realize it's just an illusion, that people are going to bring their own stuff into it."

—DAVID SEDARIS

CONTENTS

———

AUTHOR'S NOTE

———

Dear Friends and Strangers,

Welcome! I'm happy you are here.

Welcome to my musings. Welcome to my mind, my memories, and my messy life. We are about to take a journey together, and I thought we could go over the dos and don'ts of the ride. I am your storyteller but also your in-cabin flight attendant. Maybe that's a little meta but let's go with it for now. I'm not going to tell you to keep your hands and feet inside. You are in control of your own body; who am I to tell you what to do with it? If you feel like flailing about, you have my full support. I am not going to show you where the exits are. They are not clearly marked and are often hard to find. In my experience, getting in has always been easier than getting out. I won't be there to help you with your exit plan. That is completely up to you. And the reality is no matter how much support you have getting to the door, walking through is always a solo experience. Regarding seat belts, at your age, shouldn't you already know how to click it? I'm not going to insult you by telling you how, why, and when it is necessary to strap in. I am going to assume you already have that down.

Let's talk about expectations. Clarifying expectations is always a good place to start when jumping into something new. It's no fun (and never possible) to know everything; where's the adventure in that? But it is worth having some understanding of what is in these pages and, more importantly, what it is not.

I hope this book is entertaining and thought-provoking. I hope you see some of yourself in it. I hope you recognize that you are not alone, that your story is as vital as mine—that all our stories are more vital now than ever. I hope the questions I ask myself challenge you to ask yourself some of the same questions or new ones. I hope you reach out to tell me about any insights you have. I hope this collection of essays leads you to wonder—to think about how much of your identity, who you are, your personal narrative, and the words you use to describe yourself come from you. I hope you think about how many of these elements were designed by you, for you, and how many of them were created by others for their benefit.

- This isn't a self-help book. I am not here to tell you how to find yourself or give you my five-step plan to build your perfect identity. If any book you are reading tells you how to create your identity, I suggest shutting it. Loudly. To make a point. No one can tell you who you are, although almost everyone will try.
- This is a self-exploration of my own identity, a deconstruction and reconstruction within seventeen essays and four interludes. It is a journey to better understand where I come from, who I am, and why it matters to know. This

is a moment in time, a reflection of my first half-century. (Shit, when did I get old?)

- This isn't a book about how to parent a queer child. My child identifies as queer, and they are a main character in these pages. They inspired the writing of this book and are way cooler than me—but this is not a book about their story. When and if they choose to write a story about their life, I suggest you buy it. I will probably feel nervous (like the way my parents feel about this book), but I'll buy it anyway.
- This is not a sensationalized account of my struggle to adapt to my child's queer identity. No doubt I had questions and fears and other stuff we explore in these pages, but their identity is not on display here.
- My child uses they/them pronouns, which I use when referring to them. If you are not used to this, this is a perfect opportunity for you to practice. I am thrilled these pages can be a part of your journey to get comfortable with it, because you are going to need to out in the world.
- This is a collection of essays. It doesn't have to be read in order, but it helps as previous essays inform later ones. The essays are of varying length, tone, and subject matter. Some essays include stories and reflections interspersed with social commentary. Other essays or interludes remix the format for a little change of pace.
- This book is a pause in a full, busy, and complicated life. It takes a look at the path we take as parents, partners, women, and individuals, and it questions how much of it was designed for us, as opposed to by us. It is an exploration of how our identities are formed, who has the power to form them, and the impact prioritizing someone else's story of who we are over our own has on us all.

I hope that, by the end of this book, those of us who are friends are still friends and those of us who are strangers are now friends.

With Love,
Maryann

MOTHER OF A DAUGHTER

———

"Your story is what you have, what you will always
have. It is something to own."
—MICHELLE OBAMA, *BECOMING*

I am no longer the mother of a daughter. For fourteen years,
I was. Then one day, in the waiting area of New York's Penn
Station, I was informed I was not. This is an undeniably selfish way to mention my child's second coming out, but it is
nonetheless true.

We had just spent a delightful day in New York City, seeing the musical *The Prom* on Broadway. Our usual after-show
ritual includes a walk down Eighth Avenue and a stop at
Balducci's for sandwiches and copious amounts of candy,
and then our leisurely stroll continues down to Penn Station.
My husband and I had lived in New York City for ten years
before our child was born. Although it seems like a lifetime

ago, I always feel a sense of ease moving through the streets. I'm strangely comforted by the contrasts of the city. How you can feel a sense of privacy while amid all the chaos that surrounds you. How the people in the city can be equally cold and giving at the same time.

Back at Penn Station, my child shared that they didn't identify as a girl anymore and also didn't identify as a boy. I was confused and momentarily distracted because they had chosen another public place for a coming-out conversation. Their first coming out happened in the Moroccan desert while we were glamping (glamour camping). The camp included eight other families who had come from all over the world to enjoy a unique experience in the Sahara—just as we had.

Accompanying my confusion about their gender was a jumble of emotions and questions, along with an overwhelming sense of pride. The only thing that was clear to me was Penn Station didn't have enough napkins to capture the tears and snot on display from the two of us. Two years later, two wonderful celebrations occurred on January 20, 2021; the first female and first woman of color vice president was sworn in, and we celebrated the second anniversary of our Penn Station conversation.

The established rules that govern who we are supposed to be are powerful, but they are also impermanent. These rules are taught to us in overt and discrete ways. When we are born, a complicated biological process pieces together the internal and external parts that set off a wave of assumptions about who we are and what we will become. And the fervor with which those assumptions are spun up into actions that define our choices or opportunities is a problem.

Once pregnant, somehow, I just knew I was going to be the mother of a daughter. We were still living in NYC at the time, and I was walking down Broadway when it hit me. I remember it like it was yesterday. Maybe I willed it to be, but I just knew I was having a girl. It's possible my unconscious desire to figure some shit out with my mother led to my certainty. Or it could have been the mac and cheese I'd been eating for breakfast, lunch, and dinner. Either way, at roughly twenty weeks, it was confirmed with an awkward picture of our child spread eagle for the ultrasound.

The discarding of my mother-of-a-daughter narrative set off a journey of self-discovery I wasn't expecting. Out of all the navel-gazing I had anticipated exploring over time, this was not the one I had envisioned. Our status as mother and daughter was confirmed, wasn't it? Once the gender was identified fourteen years ago, there wasn't much point to reassess it, right? I happily took it for granted. It was symmetry. There was a romance to it; it was the two of us against the world. I loved the fact that the closeness my child and I shared filled a space missing in my relationship with my mother. I hadn't realized how attached I was to having a daughter. It made sense at the time, and it fed me. In hindsight, I think the narratives we hold onto the tightest are usually the ones we should disentangle first.

We are born into a world of circumstances and expectations that prescript our identity before we can even make a choice about who we are and what we want to be. There is so much about who we become that we do not choose. We do not choose our genetics, socioeconomic status, place of origin, ethnicity or race, parents' education or physical or mental health, or even our parents' desire to parent a child. Layered on top of that is a mirage of expectations perpetrated by our parents, extended family, schools, care providers, cultures, media outlets, governments and governmental systems, and societies. We stand at the center of that matrix of circumstances and expectations, trying to develop our own personal identity. An identity that encompasses our gender or sexual identity, our goals or beliefs: the things that we claim as our own.

All these circumstances and expectations weave together into stories that tell us who we are before we even think to ask ourselves the question: Who do *I* think I am? It is easy to get attached to those stories. They form this big thing called our identity. They form our sense of self, inform our relationships, and shape our roles in society. We often just accept those stories without doing the actual work to understand them. It's worth considering we are the author of some of those stories, but many of them have been created for us by others. It's good to distinguish the difference between the two. Soon after our Penn Station exchange, the questions emerged. Why was my mothering so intricately laced around the gender of my child? Why do I feel like I'm losing something? Why do others feel so invested in which bathroom my child uses? How did my child become so wise at such a young age? Why do Broadway musicals always inspire us to have deep, meaningful conversations at their conclusion?

These essays are an exploration of those questions and many more. They discuss questions that didn't make sense until I began this journey into better understanding my identity, thanks to my child's willingness to question their own. Once the floodgates opened, the questions kept coming. Why do I feel guilty for loving my single parent life? Why is being a single woman so complicated? What does it mean to be a woman in the first place? What's up with my relationship with my mother? Why do I have a hard time answering the question 'Where do you come from?' What is my origin story?

I guess, as Robert Frost wrote, the only way out is through. The only way to know is to get started.

IT'S NOT YOUR
STORY TO TELL

———

"We tell ourselves stories in order to live."

—JOAN DIDION, *THE WHITE ALBUM*

Leave it to a lactation counselor to make you feel like your inability to conjure up milk from your mammary glands is the one thing that will ruin your child's future opportunities. Maybe there are other things worse than my defective boobs, like not loving my child or leaving them to be raised by wolves, but it was clear I was failing in my parenting duties, and it was only the first twenty-four hours. Can't the lactation bully take into account that your impatient child arrived before your mammary glands had woken up from a thirty-two-year siesta?

My breastfeeding battle continued for eight weeks until I finally surrendered. My body was a battleground. I held the arrogant view that I knew my body better than my body knew itself. I was armed with advanced weaponry attached to each boob, desperate for my opponent to relent. Occasionally I made progress, filling half a bottle every couple of days. But I never made enough to feed the troops. I had to accept defeat.

During my breastfeeding ordeal, my husband didn't have anything constructive to say. Most of the time, he seemed scared of me, possibly with good reason. I wasn't about to share this particular challenge with my father, my most reliable confidante. His usually stoic advice seemed out of place in my current predicament. My mother, unfortunately, had no firsthand experience with breastfeeding. As she explained at some point after the fact, "It's just not what was done in my time. You just didn't breastfeed." With a limited number of women breastfeeding babies in the early seventies, when I was born, it made sense that my mom wasn't an expert. Now, come to think of it, maybe it's her fault that I am failing my child right now. The lactation bully was right! "The breast is best!" If only my mom had locked me to a nipple, I would be winning at parenting right now. I was left to wallow alone, half asleep, with a vacuum pump suctioned to each boob. As much as I wanted to control my mammary glands, the reality was they weren't going to do what I was telling them to do.

I was not in control.

It is possible that no sleep, the feeling of failure, the stress of not providing what my child needed, along with a pinch of postpartum depression, led those around me to look at me like I was nuts. I was a wreck, and my family didn't know what to do with me.

I have always been a person much more comfortable with action than with feelings. Feelings are necessary to inform action, but they are not to be indulged. I'm not sure how much of this point of view came from nature or nurture. My father is not much of a sharer, nor was his mother or father before him. The more you pushed my brother to express an emotion, which I was inclined to do, the quieter he got. As he has aged, he has perfected the art of using logic to deflect his feelings, much like our father. I married a man who wasn't eager to express his emotions, and when he did, they were too often laced with anger, which didn't encourage me to become more comfortable with my own.

This prioritization of action over feelings has been spectacular for fueling accomplishment in my family, but not so great for helping each other through emotional crises. My family could see I was struggling and would mutter in passing with each other, but they were mostly afraid to approach me. They just didn't know what to say or do.

My mother is a different story.

No matter how comfortable we all are with expressing our emotions, we all need to find a way to process what we are going through. Some of that processing can be done independently, internally. We may write in a diary or think it through in our heads. But it's likely at some point, we will need to share those feelings with others. To get it out of our body, out of our brain, to make sense of it all. My mother is a sharer, an external processor, with a need to share whatever she is feeling and thinking with, well… everyone. It has been a constant challenge in my brother's and my adolescent and adult life: what to tell or not tell mom, because the ladies down the street will find out about it at some point. My brother's solution was just not to say anything. Ever. To anyone. I have always struggled with the choice of how to navigate this challenge and didn't really understand the full scope of my mother's burden until I had a child of my own.

After giving up on breastfeeding, I was starting to feel better, and my mother invited me out for a mani-pedi at her salon. It was nice to venture out, enjoy a little face-to-face with other people, and the petite young woman pampering me seemed pleasant enough.

After introductions and between exfoliations, my pedicurists began, "My cousin had breast implants."

"Oh, okay," I said.

She continued, "Yeah, it was a disaster. They swelled up in a weird way. She got an infection, and they had to be taken out. It was awful."

Still not quite understanding this line of dialogue, I responded, "Oh, that's terrible. I hope she's okay."

"Yeah, you too, yeah, she's fine now. The whole ordeal didn't last as long as eight weeks, but it was still just as terrible."

It started to hit me… Is this woman trying to relate to me by using her cousin's terrible implant story? Are we about to trade boob stories? How would she even know… Wait, why did she say, "You too" and "eight weeks." I don't know this woman. How is it possible she knows… Oh, no! I looked through the salon, and there I saw her, that bright and engaging older woman, her hair full goop, able to defy nature and turn your hair any color imaginable. All I wanted to do was scream at the top of my lungs, "Mom, it is not your story to tell!" But I didn't. I fumed. I sat there in silence.

* * *

When our child was four, their father and I separated and subsequently divorced a couple years later. Divorce is a process that requires you to deconstruct your life and then rebuild it. Family relationships are tested, friendships fall away, family rituals need to be redesigned. The way you look at the world and how the world stares back at you all changes.

The time we get to spend with our children is a luxury often taken for granted. They are only young once, and youth, as it is for everyone, is fleeting. Post-divorce, it's hard to come to grips with losing control over the time you have with your child. You can't see your child when you want, where you want. Your time with them is scheduled and structured. It is an obvious, and not so obvious, revelation when you are no longer living in the same home with the person you share that child with. I knew it to be true, that I'd have to come to accept it as a necessary consequence of choosing to build the life I wanted, but learning to live with it was a new journey all its own.

Holidays. They are a challenge no matter what your family structure looks like. Pop in a divorce; it is a conundrum of who gets whom, when, and for how long.

Disillusioned and depressed at the thought of spending another holiday season alone when my child was six, we built a new Christmas routine in the shape of a trip for just the two of us, always scheduled right before Christmas. It became our favorite ritual, our gift to each other, one we looked forward to each year. Their father always had the Christmas holiday, and we always had our holiday trip. As the trips became a bit more ambitious, the time of year changed, but they were always ours, an adventure for just the two of us. We went to New York City; Washington, DC; Cologne, Germany; London; Edinburgh, Scotland; Morocco; and Oman before a global pandemic sidelined our holiday excursions.

* * *

On one of our holiday trips, my child came out to me the first time. They were thirteen. Although the location for their coming-out moment was quite spectacular, the announcement itself was a little anticlimactic. A tent somewhere in the Sahara bore witness to the moment, along with the rest of the camp at our glamping retreat. Privacy was one luxury we were *not* indulging in at the time. Therefore, their coming out and our ensuing conversation is possibly a part of someone else's story of their Moroccan vacation, as well as our own.

We arrived in the Sahara to enjoy two days of glamping. It was a spectacular time spent blissfully doing nothing surrounded by the sun and the sand. I spent hours in a hammock reading, my child running up and down the sand dunes. I watched them go from a little human in the distance to a speck on the horizon, wondering what internal adventure was playing out in their mind.

I'm not sure I handled their coming out correctly. I was supportive but not surprised, which seemed to disappoint them. After helping them find YA books with LGBTQ themes at their request, enjoying all the sketches they shared featuring same-sex pairs, and their disinterest in boys in *that* way, it wasn't a hard leap to make. We had never talked directly about their romantic or sexual preferences until that night, but they seemed on a journey toward the LGBTQ universe as far as I could tell.

When we arrived stateside, before we learned that American had canceled our flight back to DC, I called their father to let him know we had landed. As we were on the phone, I couldn't hold it in; I had to share with him the whole experience. It didn't occur to me until later that I had outed my child to their father. On a bright spring day, in the middle of the sidewalk, after holding it in for months, my child let me have it. Whereas I wouldn't dare confront my mother about sharing my traumatic breastfeeding story with her ladies, my child didn't care who witnessed their display. So there I was, on that sidewalk being schooled by my angry-at-being-outed-to-their-father thirteen-year-old. It hadn't occurred to me it wasn't my story to tell. I had placed them in the same situation my mother repeatedly put me in throughout my life. My child shoved a mirror in front of me and, with an imaginary hand on the back of my head, rubbed my nose in it hard. I felt terrible; the guilt was palpable. Peppered alongside it was a strange sensation I didn't often feel: empathy for my mother.

WHERE ARE YOU FROM?

——

"Sometimes you don't sense or understand your roots, how they make you what you are, until you've been uprooted."

—GRACE OLMSTEAD, *UPROOTED: RECOVERING*
THE LEGACY OF THE PLACES WE'VE LEFT BEHIND

When people ask me where I am from, I don't know how to answer: 23andMe tells me I'm 70 percent British and Irish and 30 percent Italian. I had a little fantasy I would click on the color-coded report, and something surprising would be revealed. Eureka! Like magic, I would be struck with new insight into who I am and where I come from. No such luck. The info was as expected, as was my uninspired feeling after clicking on the link.

When I get asked where I am from, I pivot and answer by outlining where I have lived instead. The script is as follows: "I did fourteen years in Indiana, high school outside of Baltimore, college in Michigan, then moved to Florida,

New York City, Massachusetts, and then to the District of Columbia where I live now." Recently after reciting my script, the young man sitting across from me smiled and asked, "Where did you do 'your time' in Indiana?" It took me a second, but I chuckled, and we continued down the path of getting to know each other. I certainly don't look back at my time in Indiana as a sentence of some kind, but I appreciated his insight into my choice of words. The words we use to tell our stories matter, and they let us and others know what we think, even if we haven't figured it out for ourselves.

I often wonder what people really want to know when asking where I'm from. It's often a gateway question in the life-hack list for getting to know someone. Most of the time, it is a casual conversation starter, and there is nothing wrong with that. It is a relevant question, but it can be given too much weight as a definer for who we are. Maybe I feel that way as a defense mechanism because of my disconnection from the places I have lived.

Getting to know someone and connecting with them shouldn't be distilled down to the answers to a couple quick questions. It is arrogant to think we know someone based on our determination of their ethnicity, gender, age, and their answers to our initial questions that are designed to distill their class, upbringing, education, and political or social affiliations. The answers either solve correctly or incorrectly the equation designed to figure out if they belong or not.

Even asking the question, depending upon who is doing the asking and who it is directed toward, can illustrate a bias. I get that some quick determination is inevitable, but I'd love to switch up the questions now and then. Toss in a "What are you passionate about?" or "What led you to the work you are doing?" This answer tells me what inspires you, whether you are mission-driven or motivated by another source. Or how about, "How long have you lived in [pick the place]?" Here I can gauge your commitment to the environment: Are you here to stay or just passing through? I also like, "What have you been reading or watching lately that you are excited about, or what do you do for fun?" This attempts to find out if you will actually like the person and want to invite them to happy hour or not. You can even ask, "What are the first fifteen numbers of pi?" if the spirit moves you. If you are desperate to ask, "Where are you from?" try "Where do you call home?" instead. For me, the script for that one is easy: "Wherever my child and I are."

* * *

Over ten years ago, post-divorce, my boyfriend at the time had just hightailed it for the hills. Distraught, I responded as any heartbroken woman would: I cut off all my hair and bought a dog. My ex-husband and I had owned two Great Dane rescues, so I wanted a large and loveable dog. Boo is all that. A mutt. A hound dog, maybe a little greyhound or collie, so we imagined. It was hard to decipher the combination of breeds that have turned him into the beauty he is. Boo is strong, sleek, loving, and so happy to have a home—a couple qualities I wish the ex-boyfriend had possessed. He is also a hunter, eagerly capturing and torturing any accessible rodent around the property, then presenting the mangled thing to me with pride. Boo is a great dog.

My mother, wicked cool lady that she is, does not enjoy uncertainty. The unspecific genealogy of Boo didn't cut it for her. Luckily, not only can you clearly identify your heritage, but you can also decipher your dog's indeterminate lineage thanks to DNA testing. Drum roll, please. Post DNA test, we now know Boo's daddy was 100 percent redbone coonhound, and his mom was a yellow Labrador retriever who mated with a Maltese. The first half of the recipe makes perfect sense; the second half requires a minute to picture. Google it if it will help. Certainly not what one would expect for a mated pair.

But so what? More power to them. Who are we to judge? Love, elusive and rare as it can be, should be honored however and wherever it presents itself. I don't love Boo any more or less knowing his roots. In the online dating age, we have some perceived power that we can point and click ourselves to the perfect mate. Do you think Boo's mom would have ever swiped right on her Maltese lover? He's too short and stocky, his tail is too fluffy, too hairy, and not the right color. One of those items would have knocked him off the list. If that had happened, my child and I would have lost out on the perfect dog. My dad, who adores Boo, would have lost out on his canine soulmate. My mom would have lost out on her late-in-life child. What a shame that would have been.

When I think about my evasive answer to the question of where I am from, I wonder what knowing the list of places I've lived tells you about who I am. Feeling untethered by place, I have always felt like I could live anywhere. The people and the opportunity are what draw me and keep me in a new environment. My lack of attachment to place has left me wildly agile and adaptable but also somewhat rootless.

I have always envied people with deep roots to the places they have lived. I have a colleague whose family has lived for six generations in Washington, DC. My best friend's family and most of her childhood friends still live in the same town in Ohio. They each have deep relationships with friends and family that are anchored in experiences that are tied to the place they live. They go home and are immediately a part of the community that exists in that town, a part of those memories, tied to those people. I have found it hard to maintain relationships with the people I grew up with because I never returned to the place where those relationships were developed. When I was going off to college, my parents moved again, so when I returned for holidays, I was arriving at a new house and working to get to know a new community. The constant was family, and the constant was change. When I would come home, the town, house, and community had changed, but the family was still the same. And as my father always says, "You never look back."

There is a deep Italian ethnic history on my father's side. When I think about the choices my immigrant great-grandparents made to leave Italy for Brooklyn, I romanticize a kind of ethnic and cultural connectedness that seems so foreign to me. For most of my life, I have never really thought about my ethnic heritage. I knew I was Italian, Irish, and, as I was told, "a bunch of other stuff." Of course, now I know not so much "other stuff"—pretty much just northwestern and southern European. On my first trip to Italy, a group hiking excursion through the Dolomites, my Italian ancestors never crossed my mind while wandering around the northern Italian Alps. A couple days into the trip, I was at lunch with one of my fellow hikers and a local older couple we had met at the café. We were sitting shoulder to shoulder, in the middle of a family-style table that ended at a window looking out to a small cobblestone street. The clientele seemed an interesting mix of travelers and locals sporting that light look of annoyance at those of us passing through.

We were having a pleasant but somewhat stilted conversation about the day-to-day. At some point, my fellow hiker asked,

"Maryann, you're Italian, aren't you? Your last name is Lombardi, right? Or was that your husband's name?" As a freshly divorced woman on her first solo trip and annoyed at the assumption, I directed the conversation away from *husband*-like things and said, "Yes, my father's family came from Italy." The older couple perked up and asked, "Where were they from? Do you know where they lived?" I responded the way any self-respecting woman pushing forty would and said, "Not sure, I'd have to ask my mom." I texted her, and she responded quickly.

One of the many wonderful things about my mother is she knows everything: geography, history, fun facts, annoying facts, stuff about birds, literally every ailment every family member has had for generations, or the service record of the guy sitting next to her on the airplane. She was our search engine before being usurped by Google. When I shared the name of the town my grandparents came from with the older Italian couple, they looked at each other and then told me matter-of-factly, "You come from an ugly place." I wasn't exactly sure what to do with that information. I didn't think it was possible for anywhere in Italy to be ugly. Could it be that *Frommer's* had lied to me? Years later, after relaying the story to a very cute history and culture professor I met at a Starbucks, he wondered whether "ugly" had been a reference to the cultural and social environment of the town, not the aesthetics. It seems the area was well known for its connection to the Cosa Nostra, the Italian mafia.

When I think back to that moment, being told I come from an ugly place, I feel like I should have been offended. I should have felt something, anything except the disconnection I was sitting with. I was interested in what they said, noticed the judgment on their faces and in the tone of their voices, but I couldn't make the connection. They were insulting my great-grandparents, and that insult traveled the direct line to me. They were insulting me. Yet, I felt nothing.

The more I think about my Italian roots, dig into the family history, hear the stories, and read about the culture, the more curious I become. But it doesn't make me feel like I know myself any better. My DNA tells me that I am 70 percent northwestern European/British and Irish and 30 percent Southern European/Italian. But my EBI (Experience Based Identity) these past forty-nine years tells me I am 28 percent Indiana, 20 percent New York City, 16 percent Massachusetts, 16 percent DC, and a bunch of other stuff. I may not feel connected to place or even know anyone who resides in that 28 percent or 20 percent anymore, but there is no denying that the experiences I had and the connections I made at the time made me who I am today.

* * *

My father's motto is you don't look back. Sometimes I think about the image of the rearview mirror, and those "objects [that] are closer than they appear," and I wonder if those objects wouldn't loom so large if we just turned around and stared at them now and then. As a family, we were always moving forward, whether physically moving from one place to another or being out and about doing something. If you get hurt or injured, you get up, brush it off, and walk on. If you attempt something scary, you ask yourself if you could handle the worst thing that could happen, and if so, you jump in. I'm not mad at it—it was a pretty great childhood. There was not much to complain about: a heck of a lot of love, support, presence, and resilience training. But there wasn't a lot of time spent on reflection.

The more I think about my time in Indiana, the more I realize how impactful the 28 percent was. Many of my lifelong passions and my foundations stem from there. My love of animals—my first true love being a horse named Sunny. My obsession with music. The need to feel connected to people. The discovery that the wrong group of people can ruin a great idea. The root of them all began in Indiana. I can remember wasting many afternoons on horseback, napping on Sunny's back while he grazed in a field. The luxury of it, the simplicity. Or running up and down the backstage steps of the Indiana University Opera House as a *Midsummer Night's Dream* fairy painted in green and white, giggling with my friends as we awaited our entrance. I remember being surrounded by thinkers, always welcome but reminded to listen now and talk later. I watched my parents' ability to build community together, albeit in very different ways. All those feelings, those discoveries that have turned to passions, my core beliefs—I can trace back to Indiana. So, although I feel a loss not having any connection to the place and the people in Bloomington, the more I think about it, I feel deeply connected to what I learned and how that made me the person I am.

So maybe the disconnection from the physical place is inevitable for some; it was for me. Can I declare roots in a place I have been uprooted from? If I am of a group of people who creative economist Richard Florida defines as mobile, who have the education and means to move to places with greater opportunities, what does that mean for where I come from? The only thing I do know is I am the mother of my child, the daughter of John and Cathryn, the sister of John. I am a cousin, a parent, a community builder, a storyteller, a friend, a lover, an entrepreneur, a seeker, and a lifelong learner. And maybe I am also from Indiana.

THE SOUND OF SILENCE

———

"You have a grand gift for silence, Watson. It makes
you quite invaluable as a companion."
—'THE MAN WITH THE TWISTED LIP'
INCLUDED IN THE BOOK *THE ADVENTURES OF*
SHERLOCK HOLMES BY SIR ARTHUR CONAN DOYLE

My Aunt Luciana was seven years old when her mother, Mary
Ellen, died. My father was five. Shortly after, my grandfather remarried, and Janice became my father and Luciana's
mother. Subsequently, under the edict from my grandfather,
no one spoke of Mary Ellen again. The year was 1949.

Losing her birth mother had a deep impact on my aunt.
She was old enough to remember her; my father did not.
Luciana was originally named after her birth mother, Mary
Ellen. She changed her name to Luciana years later because
she said Mary meant "Queen of Sorrows." But I think there
must have been more to it than that. She was an artist and
a scholar who struggled to come to terms with her identity

and declared war on anyone or anything that dared define it for her.

Luciana was a passionate and complicated woman. My memories of her are episodic and appear more like a word cloud than a fully realized person. She was tall, a bit severe in stature, and quite beautiful as a younger woman. If ever eager to hide her opinion on a subject, her face betrayed her instantly. Subtlety was not her friend, nor her enemy, only an uncomfortable acquaintance that popped by every now and then. I had the luxury of spending more time with her during the last year of her life, as her mind began to fail her. But for most of my memory, she was difficult and complex.

I have this fragment of a memory of being confined in an elevator with Luciana and my mother, watching a tense exchange between the two of them. It's a strange memory that just sits there with no context but is vivid nonetheless. Mainly I see my mother's face, layered in frustration and suppression. My experience of my mother, especially in my youth, was not one of suppression, so this was exciting. *How did that happen?* I think as I imagine the complicated emotional gymnastics that made that moment possible for my mother. I would watch Luciana manage her frustration with my mother, with my brother and me, with a circumstance, with the environment, and with the way the world may have moved around her. Listening to my father talk about his older sister, it is clear he loved her deeply, protected her, and looked up to her. He appreciated her gifts and accepted her unconditionally in a way I imagine no one else did. Ever. And those who loved him found ways to love her, too, even if we didn't always understand her.

As a child, my observation of Luciana was filtered through my adolescent brain and spit out as judgment—"She's mean" or "She's no fun"—but I look back on that time and am disappointed in myself for not caring more to get to know her. In hindsight, I see her behavior and her gifts as something compelling, and the causal connections between our lives have meaning. We both share being the only two members of our family ever divorced. She was a bit more ambitious by divorcing twice but we still share the membership. We were/are both creatives. We were/are both wildly independent. We were/are both combative against the expectations of others and drove/are driving toward a life that means something to us. And both of us, at times, have felt like we don't fit into our family.

My child had the opportunity to get to know Luciana a little bit. They would chat on the phone, have these awkward conversations, and sometimes sit in silence for a touch too long, but then after the conversation was over, my child would hang up the phone unbothered. They didn't mind. They were more patient with her, with the moments, than I was. Maybe Luciana and my similarities made those kinds of moments improbable.

Silence can be a powerful tool for healing and self-awareness, but it can also be a weapon of suppression. Silence is as much an expression as is sound. Sometimes I imagine Luciana fighting to be heard about anything and everything over the cacophony of silence about just one thing—the absence of Mary Ellen: the abundance of thoughts and feelings cascading over the missing pictures, the absent stories, and items that usually accompany a life lived. But her father's edict was absolute, and it was all gone. All of it was made more unimaginable with the inclusion of Mary Ellen's mother and sister as an active part of the family. My grandfather's power was unquestioned: it wasn't that you wouldn't speak of Mary Ellen in his presence; you just wouldn't speak of her at all.

I didn't know my grandfather well, but I loved him dearly. In my memory, he is a tall and serious man: his height imposing, his manner quiet and attentive. We would walk, sometimes in a comfortable silence, but mostly chatting about something, chatting about anything. I remember so clearly how it felt to be around him. He had this ability to calm me and to make me feel like I mattered. I didn't have to prove myself or fight for focus. I just had to be present and discuss something, whether mundane or profound—either was appropriate. When I was with him on those walks, I always had 100 percent of his attention.

My grandfather was first-generation Italian American and the only child of Maria and Giovanni. He never met his birth father. At thirty-two, Giovanni, born in that "ugly" town in Italy, left Maria a widow at twenty years of age. She was about to give birth to her first baby—my grandfather. Soon after, Maria married Giacomo and had another seven children. The story of Giacomo is spotty and peppered with words like "drunk," "absent," and "ineffective." It *was* clear it was left to my grandfather to do the work of providing for the family at a very young age, which he did, reluctantly, becoming the Don of a large, extended, Italian American family, none of whom shared his last name.

I never had the opportunity to see my grandfather in that environment, surrounded by his half-siblings and other family members. But I did see how they reacted to my father the couple times we visited them all in Brooklyn as a family. There was this residual feeling of gratefulness and respect that seemed to be passed down from my grandfather to my father by those aunts and uncles. I didn't understand it; it certainly wasn't explained to me at the time, but it was clearly visible.

During the one interview my father gave me on this subject of his father, he explained:

"The only thing I know about my father is mostly what my aunts taught me. And there were things he did that validated what they said. He was raised by his mother as far as we know. And he was in charge of all the kids. We don't know what happened between his birth and practically the end of his high school. We have no information. We have no feedback. We have no gossip. We have no family conversations that focus on that formative period in which he emerged as the support of the family. We don't know that, because he wouldn't tell.

"Where they were, they were all Italians there, in that community, everybody's connected. Everything's Italian; the communities Italian, the churches are Italian, the school is Italian, and everybody speaks in Italian. The story in my reconstruction of it—which is incomplete and probably inaccurate—but as he grew older, the large extended Italian community creates for him the opportunities to work hard to generate money to support a family that has a breadwinner who is not effective. Whether he was helping in the bakery business, or in the grocery store, or he became involved in the garment industry as a cutter. He worked there for a long time. He had all of these connections to businesses in the area where he was a worker at a very low level.

"So he becomes the primary, at some point in time, and becomes responsible for organizing the activities of the people that were connected to his mother. I don't know why it was him and not some uncle or somebody else who was older or more significant, but there was no way to ever supplant him. My aunts would tell me, 'We know a lot, we're gonna tell you more. He doesn't want us to tell you about it.' But they never did."

* * *

The choices we make and the people we become do not happen in isolation. They are fueled by our circumstances, our environment, and ultimately our intentions. We are products of a time and a place and take actions that represent that. If we don't take that into account, gazing from the safe distance time provides can lead us to make unfair assumptions about the choices others have taken.

Looking back, I have been trying to understand the silence that was passed down on my father's side of the family. I am trying to move beyond the simple answer of, "It was just the way things were done back then." It was overt, like a neighbor who was never invited inside the house but was left outside ringing the doorbell. Known but never spoken of. My father and Luciana were surrounded by people who could tell the family stories, fill in the gaps, hinted at doing so but would not. They lived with their father, who could have shared his own story, but he did not.

Author Lois Lowry writes in the young adult dystopian novel *The Giver* that "the worst part of holding the memories is not the pain. It's the loneliness of it. Memories need to be shared." I think about my grandfather and how lonely it must have been to hold on to all those memories himself. For anyone who holds it all inside, it must be terribly lonely. Much of what I learned about my grandfather's childhood (and my father's, for that matter) was from fragments my mother shared. She was able to piece together things through genealogical research, conversations, and being patient and willing to ask questions. Thankfully, my father has become chattier as he has aged. I have also become more comfortable with asking, poking, and pestering. Maybe since my dad has slowed down, retired, stopped moving so fast—maybe there is more room for those stories to surface.

I didn't really think about the impact of this silence until I was much older. It's hard to feel an absence when you don't know that something is missing. There were some stories. I would watch my mother and her sister sit in stitches rattling off stories of their youth from their father or their travel adventures. I would see my dad at the table with his loyal colleagues telling past tales of the political and academic battlefields. I even remember the last time my dad, mom, and I visited the Brooklyn relatives together—the closest the relatives came to spilling the beans was reminding my father of the last time they saw my grandfather at the brownstone. It took me a while to realize that aside from the stories of my mother's youth, the storytelling I witnessed was a replay of only the most recent memories, as if there were a past-due date on anything that happened in my father's or grandfather's youth.

I can imagine there were benefits for my grandfather not replaying the difficulties of his youth. Silence can be adaptive and help us move forward. From a young age, my grandfather had responsibilities to earn for the family and keep the family together. His silence could have helped him stay focused on what needed to be done to support his mother and steps-iblings as a young man. That learned behavior could have helped him navigate the pain of his loss as a widowed father of two young children. It could have helped him support a new wife and mother and incorporate her into the family. Not reviewing and recalling the stories and experiences can allow the painful feelings to be let go. To be lost. But silence unchecked can balloon to have a life of its own.

Luciana was not silent. One of the many compelling elements of her story is the fact that she documented it through her words, through her experiences, and her expressions— she felt it, explored it, and shared it. She wrote it down in letters she sent her father and mother, letters she sent my father and mother; she shared her pain, conflict, disillusionment. She shared pieces of her struggle. Although it isn't a full record of her life, for a family that valued leaving the past in its place, the sound visible in those pages and her experiences, the sound that reverberates in my dad's memory of his sister, feels revolutionary.

* * *

Silence can be inherited. From our earliest days as children, we watch, and we absorb. The behavior that allows silence to grow and take root. It can be mimicked. It can be learned. My dad has inherited it, that silence, as has my brother. Although diluted, in ways I have as well. I understand the desire to erase what came before in order to avoid pain and move on. I'm quite good at it. I don't hold onto physical stuff that reminds me of hard times. I let go easily of people who have not had my best interests at heart or who have been unkind. My attraction to change helps me leave behind difficulties I really don't want to address. I'm also a hard-core text deleter. In some ways this is pretty darn healthy; in others, it is an avoidance mechanism for limiting the everyday pain of living.

I don't pretend to understand the cultural dynamic or the challenge my grandfather faced as a young man providing for his mother and extended family, or the personal pressures he faced as a single father in the 1940s. Nor can I understand the cultural and gender dynamics or the circumstances that led Mary Ellen's mother to abide by my grandfather's directive. It's myopic to make assumptions based on the limited information I have. But it's painful to think about. It's painful to sit in the contradiction of loving the memory of someone so much but also be disappointed in their actions. I try to reconcile the choices they made with the impact the choice of silence has had on so many.

So many people have to fight to be seen and scream to be heard. Their presence is seen as problematic for any number of reasons, and therefore they have been erased. From families. From history. This has been the case for the gender-nonconforming community for generations. My child lives in privileged circumstances with a family that is loving, with a friend network that is supportive, in a city that is welcoming. This shouldn't be a privilege, but it unfortunately is. This should be the norm.

I have been on enough emails about my child's queer friends needing support because someone's family has cast them out. Or teachers and adults refuse to use preferred pronouns, which actively ignores and silences the kid standing in front of them. It doesn't take much work to find the states that are passing anti-trans laws to eliminate opportunity and access for kids like my own. It is undeniably terrible that one of the deciding factors about where my child goes to college is the potential for violence against the trans community in the city and state that college is based in. It is scary enough to send your child off into the world alone; add the layer of gender nonconformity, and it's downright terrifying.

For too many, it's easier to silence those who swim against the current than navigate the discomfort necessary for acceptance and understanding. Archeologist Gabby Omoni Hartemann states, "The erroneous idea that we, transgender people, 'have no past,' feeds the notion held by many cisgender people that we don't belong in the present." It would be easier if my child conformed to the gender they were assigned at birth—if they were not the authentic person they are. They have told me so, which is a gut-wrenching thing to hear your child say. But, thankfully, they have not inherited silence. Thankfully, they are not taking that easy path they speak of.

We know almost nothing about my dad's birth mother. Those who could tell the story of her life didn't, and therefore she is gone. I wish I had asked my grandfather about Mary Ellen on one of our walks. If I had known she existed at the time, maybe I would have. Or maybe not. Who knows. If I had, I wonder what he would have said. Unfortunately, Mary Ellen's story is not mine to tell, but I really wish it was told to someone, so it could have been told to me. So I could tell it to my child. So it would not be lost to history. I wish I had made the effort to get to know Luciana better while she was alive. To ask her about her time in Brazil, to commiserate about the challenges of marriage and divorce, to talk about feminism in art and music, one of her scholarly interests—to ask her what she remembered about Mary Ellen. If I had, I wonder what she would have said.

DEAR DIARY, IT'S NOT YOU, IT'S ME

"Anytime you want to call, I'll be happy to talk. Writing about what's happening seems to engrave the experiences in concrete, and I am moving through them, so don't want to get stuck describing them!"

—MY AUNT, LUCIANA LOMBARDI

(FROM A LETTER SENT TO MY MOTHER IN 1973)

Dear Diary,

I have failed you. It's not you. It's me. You have lain patiently on my bedside table, on the bookshelf, and in my dresser drawer for years and years. I have wanted to participate in the opportunity you provide. To share my day-to-day, my feelings, and my rants and raves. But the truth is I like the image of you more than the reality. I don't want to write down my thoughts and feelings. I don't want to read to remember. I want to experience and allow what fades to fade and what stays to stay. I recognize there is a great risk to this, but it is who I am, who I have been. Feeling the feels are hard enough, but capturing them, replaying them, sucks. I'd rather not. My apologies, but it has to be this way. It isn't fair to lead you on anymore, to have you lie there without any attention or affection. I need to accept what I know to be true and let you go. I would like to say this hurts me more than it hurts you, but that isn't the truth. I feel better already just by making the decision. And in the long run, it is probably best for both of us. My hope is by placing you in this box for the library sale that you will find someone who can appreciate you for the blank canvas you are. Can share with you their hopes and dreams. Drip their day-to-day for you to soak up and protect from anyone who dares pry. And my hope for myself is to appreciate who I am and not hold onto things that remind me of who I am not. And I am not one who writes in a diary.

ASK AND YOU SHALL RECEIVE

—

"The best scientists and explorers have the attributes of kids! They ask questions and have a sense of wonder. They have curiosity. 'Who, what, where, why, when, and how!' They never stop asking questions, and I never stop asking questions, just like a five-year-old."
—MARINE BIOLOGIST AND EXPLORER SYLVIA EARLE

To describe my mother as strong feels incomplete. She rides her strength and vulnerability like a seesaw, one overpowering the other depending on the balance of the day. She is a powerful, beautiful, and complicated woman who comes from a family of storytellers. From what I remember of her father, he could spin a yarn. His tales were tall and would get you into trouble if you took them as truth as I did in elementary school when telling my class that I was a descendant of a

Native American princess. He was romantic, warm, friendly, although unfortunately, a little distant in my memory.

My memories of my mother's mom are a bit less romantic. She was cold and quieter. She did love her "stories," though; I remember sitting with her watching the soap opera *Days of Our Lives*. She would occasionally help me out by explaining what was going on and who was with whom. To this day, when I see a promo or hear that memorable "... So are the days of our lives," I can't help but think of her.

My mother and her sister, three years her junior, can sit for hours in each other's presence just telling stories. They are who FaceTime was invented for. I find this equally exhausting and intoxicating. I can see how much that time and those stories mean to each of them, how much it matters. Those stories are their living history, and these two women have lived very interesting lives. There is a connection between the two of them that transcends their husbands and children. It is not that they haven't experienced conflict, but they are connected as sisters, no matter what. The last time I saw my aunt was at a family wedding. She made some side comment to me about how I needed to be nice to my mother. I didn't remember being *not* nice to my mother at some recent moment. No matter what led her to that comment, either the crap I put my mom through as a teenager or a more recent insensitivity, it was clear she had my mother's back.

We all capture our moments and experiences in pictures and video, but it can never replace the need to share stories with each other. When you are in a room together and connect face to face, you reinvent the story as you reshare, and it comes alive again. This is the conundrum. For those who want to forget, it is impossible if the stories live on through the people they are around. For those who want to remember, they need the space and the people with whom to share. Without the story, your story, our story, we fade away like Marty McFly's family picture in *Back to the Future*.

Our memories are selective and inexact. No matter how clear a memory is, there is no way to replay it exactly as it happened. These memories of our personal and family histories, and the experiences that design them, are what make us who we are. They are incredibly important and allow us to choose who we become. Remembering what we experience and how we feel about that is essential to our identity. Today we are able to capture and curate our lives in ways that were unimaginable in my youth and that of our parents. This curation creates a highlight reel of life activities that can be beautiful but can also distract us from the work of remembering on our own.

* * *

Starting from when my mother was ten, she lived a structured life inside the grounds of a cotton plant on the Mexican side of the Mexico-California border. My grandfather was the assistant manager of the plant. A section on the grounds included a house for the manager, a Mexican man, his wife, and two children, and another assistant manager and his wife, also from Mexico. My grandfather, grandmother, mom, and aunt lived next to them and were the only American family living on the grounds. The adobe houses were clustered around each other, with a large rectangular pool in front and a dried piece of land a bit further out that used to be a small, three-hole golf course.

The compound was enclosed with a huge chain-link fence with razor wire all around it. As you approached the compound, a guard with a large gun would greet you at the gatehouse to let you in. My mother and her sister could explore inside the compound, play with each other, swim in the pool, and get dirty—many of the essential elements of an everyday childhood. Going outside the grounds required an escort.

My mom's daily routine included at least two trips across the border, one to attend school in California, the other to head home to Mexico. The manager of the plant had children, but they were younger, and the other assistant manager didn't have any children. Friend connections made outside the grounds of the plant were made at school. Playdates and get-togethers had to be scheduled and organized on the US side of the border, and at-home adventures were limited to inside the grounds. On the weekends, the family would cross the border and visit the country club, which my grandfather designed. It wasn't a "big, hoity-toity fancy country club," as my mother made very clear to me, but it did have a nice golf course. My mom and her sister had free rein of the place as their parents would spend the day traveling the eighteen holes. The girls would play golf and tennis, swim any chance they got, and help the golf pros bag tees in the back of the pro shop.

The 1950s and 1960s, during my grandfather's tenure at the plant, saw a fair amount of labor disputes that impacted life on the grounds. Conflicts were common; union upheaval was a regular occurrence. My mother explained, "I do remember one time when we had to be evacuated from the compound. We were all in Calexico, and Dad didn't come for quite a while. And then my friend's father, who was one of the other managers, didn't come all night because he got trapped inside the compound. They had stayed to run down the hydrogen cracking station because one of the steps of making shortening out of cottonseed oil is to hydrogenate it. You see that on the label like Crisco. You have to have hydrogen to do that. It's very explosive. And there were lots of guns, lots of gunfire, and so they had to get that cracking station totally down. So any stray shot wouldn't hit it and blow it up, because if it did, it would have blown up half the town of Mexicali."

When my mother was twelve, she and my aunt were the targets of a kidnapping plot during one of the worker revolts. She still remembers it vividly. They were swept out of school for a week and taken to San Diego. En route, they stopped at a federal building, and, since American children were at risk, the FBI got involved. After a couple days, her father showed up and explained the perpetrators were caught by the Mexican police. He mentioned later that the perpetrators were "taken out to the desert," which he said was not uncommon at the time.

* * *

When I imagine the structure surrounding my mother's day-to-day as a young child and the potential for violence, a lot of my mother's demands on my actions make more sense. Control and order provide her the kind of comfort, support, and nurturing that made me run from the room screaming when directed at me. Back in the day, we were combustible, not unlike those stray bullets that could hit that cracking station if you weren't careful. I can imagine the complicated feelings it brought up in my mother's mothering me. A sparky, independent, and determined child. One disinterested in rules and regulations on principle, whether they were reasonable or not. I never found a wall I couldn't go through, and my brother never found a wall he couldn't go around.

It took me forty-nine years to directly ask my mother about her childhood, to learn the story of the kidnapping plot. My lack of curiosity about my own family seems antithetic to who I am as a person. I have always been curious and a life-long learner. It is a big part of my identity. I'm endlessly interested in people's stories and have built a career by listening to those stories and building community and opportunities for the people I serve. My mission is centered on a desire to let people know they matter. A lot of that is done by seeking out their stories and listening to their needs, and seeing how I can help. How has my curiosity not extended to my own family? What has been so hard about asking questions of them, of my mother?

Sometimes the way we see ourselves, the narrative we hold onto or present to the world, may not be consistent with the actions we take. Can I claim the label of curious if I'm not actually fully committed to practicing it? Can I be a lifelong learner when I'm not learning anything?

Young kids are masters at asking questions. If they want to know something, they will go right to the source. I was on the metro recently, and an older blind man got on the train a couple stops after me. He sat down near the door, and a child, I'm guessing six, asked,

"Hi, mister, are you blind?"

To which he replied, "Yes, I am."

"Can you see anything?" she continued.

"Not really, just some light and shapes sometimes," he said.

"That's weird."

"Maybe not weird, but different."

"How do you move around? Where is your dog?" she continued.

"I don't have a dog. I have this cane and can use it to help me."

"I wish you had a dog."

"Me too."

Kids just ask. They are unconcerned about things like comfort. The girl just asked, and the older gentleman seemed happy to be in conversation. She soaked up the information provided, processed it to some extent, and as she left, said goodbye to him, telling him she hoped he got a dog someday.

My mother is also not afraid to ask questions. She is curiosity personified. She starts with, "What are you doing? Where are you going? Who are you going to meet?" moves on, "Can you pick up this thing? Why did you pick up *that* thing? Oh, that is interesting; how are you going to use that? Did you know so and so has gout? Do you think my grand-child would like this?"

"I don't know, why don't you call *them* and ask?" I respond, exasperated. On visits, I was still sneaking out of the house as a grown-ass adult to grab coffee, trying to avoid a question before I started my day. I have learned to appreciate (and tolerate) the questions over time. I know this is one of the many ways my mother shows she loves you, that you matter, and your presence is appreciated. She asks you questions. She wants to know you. It is also how she gets control over her discomfort by being in the know.

My mother is desperate to understand her grandchild. She is trying to get a handle on the whole pronoun thing and is about 75 percent there. But she is so worried about doing or saying the wrong thing to her grandchild that she asks me all the questions swimming in her head. Then she processes it all. Mostly with people who are *not* her grandchild. She would benefit from channeling her inner six-year-old and going directly to the source.

Often we don't ask the question because we are either uninterested in the answer or afraid of the impact of the answer. I am wildly interested in my mother, in the answer to any of the questions as long as they have nothing to do with gout—and birds, I'm not really interested in birds. So what have I been afraid of? Our own ignorance is a comfortable place to lay our heads. If we just maintain the story we are accustomed to and stick with what we think we know, we don't have to challenge our assumptions based on those stories. If we have already constructed the narrative in our heads based on what makes us the most comfortable, what is the incentive to change it?

Social psychologist Adam Grant says, "Part of the problem is cognitive laziness. Some psychologists point out that we're mental misers: we often prefer the ease of hanging on to old views over the difficulty of grappling with new ones. Yet, there are also deeper forces behind our resistance to rethinking. Questioning ourselves makes the world more unpredictable. It requires us to admit that the facts may have changed, that what was once right may now be wrong. Reconsidering something we believe deeply can threaten our identities, making it feel as if we're losing a part of ourselves."

If I ask my mother about her childhood, I need to allow those new stories to rewrite what I know about her and how I feel about her. I need to rethink how I frame my relationship with her and allow our story to develop. It's simpler to maintain the narratives I have held onto for most of my life. To maintain my identity as one who is combustible with my mother. To maintain my identity as my father's daughter. To confirm she doesn't understand me the way he does—which isn't true. My mother does understand me in ways my father will never. It is understandable how we can stay locked in the parent and child dynamics of our youth, in believing the way we started is the way we continue and the way we end. But that need not be the case. Why does that one narrative, that one component of my identity, preclude me from changing it, preclude any of us from changing? I don't lose any part of my identity by getting to know my mother better. All I do is gain. We all do. We all gain by getting to know each other better, by loosening our grip on the narratives that confine our way of thinking.

If my mom asks questions of her grandchild and gets to know them better, they will co-create a narrative that benefits them both for years to come. They already have a closer relationship than I ever did with both my grandmothers simply based on the time they have spent together, which is beautifully enviable. It can be uncomfortable to ask questions, to admit you don't know, don't understand—especially when it comes to elements of identity and gender, race, belief, or another topic. But discomfort is no excuse for not trying, especially with those you care for. These questions are an act of love. It's easy to say you love someone, but it's more complicated to do the work of caring about them. Love is a tricky word. In its passive form, it is just a feeling. In its active form, it is a feeling and an action. The latter is much more powerful and sustainable than the former. The act of loving someone requires you to get to know them, to ask them, to make that effort to understand them.

To really get to know my mother, I need to not just love her but do the work of loving her. The same is true of my mother and her grandchild. The same is true for all of us.

MY FATHER'S DAUGHTER

—

"It is a common thing to be overly impressed by and attached to masks, either some mask of one's own or the mana-masks of others."

—AUTHOR AND ACADEMIC JOSEPH CAMPBELL

My dad is fifty-two.

Not really, but he is supposed to be. For a good part of my life, I have felt that fifty-two is the appropriate age for a dad, no younger and no older. Dads should stay at that age for years and years and years. At some point, they may die. Then you are super sad, but you are too distraught to really think about how a fifty-two-year-old (who lived about eighty-some years) could have croaked, so you just accept it, let it go, and grieve. Why? Because dads are supposed to be fifty-two.

For most of my life, I have not been able to remember my dad's birthday. I knew the month, clearly had no interest in the year, and would mix up the day, having to call my mom to confirm. Our brains are pretty spectacular little machines, always willing to help us forget the stuff that would require us to remember the things we don't want to. To know my dad's birthday would require me to accept that he's old. And who wants to do that? As I have been more aggressively approaching the appropriate age for a dad, I have had to get over it. Thanks to my terrible sex education class in school, I know it is not biologically possibly for my dad and me to be the same age, so I've had to get over my memory lapse. For the past couple of years, I've suddenly been able to remember the date and year of his birthday just fine. Time passes, and age happens whether we want it to or not. We can lock ourselves to memories and stories from the past, but in doing so we tend to miss the moments happening right in front of us. I know my dad better now at seventy-nine than I did when he was fifty-two, and I am thankful for that.

* * *

I am my father's daughter, but what does that mean? There is something archetypal about it. Daughters are supposed to look up to their fathers; fathers are supposed to be in conflict with their sons. Sons are supposed to be closer to their mothers and mothers in competition with their daughters. It's a story that has been told for generations. It's a story that families can adhere to in some ways, whether it's authentic or not. I wonder if the archetype is driven by the family dynamics or whether the family dynamics are driven by the archetype. Either way, I blame Sophocles and Freud.

I have always claimed to be my father's daughter. It is comfortable, and it feels true. Our similarities and differences balance each other in ways I believe to be complementary. I take pride in that. His calm, no-bullshit, unflappable nature gave room for his curious, impatient, strong-willed, emotional child to grow. If he felt fear, he didn't show it. If he worried about my choices, he never shared that. He let me be whatever and feel however I chose to.

In some ways, my dad's and mom's reactions to me were in contrast to each other. Where my mom tried to confine, my dad released, and I was drawn to the feeling of freedom I have always felt around him. I have a lot more sympathy for my mom now, looking back. My parents have always been a powerful pair, in ways that are quite spectacular, but Mom ruled the home. She did the work of day-to-day parenting and homemaking and Dad had it easy—and my dad and my relationship, at times, undermined my mom's authority.

It's odd to identify yourself in relation to another. That you are someone else's something. When I think about it in the abstract, there is a muddy undertone of possession and ownership to it that feels yucky. As if the daughter I am is designed by the father I have. In some ways, it is, but that is never the full story. It is only a piece of it.

When we primarily define ourselves by our relationship to others, what do we claim as our own? By saying I am my father's daughter, I prioritize my father's identity over mine and center myself in my role as his daughter. If we primarily introduce ourselves as someone else's wife or husband or partner, we do the same thing. When I always introduce myself as my child's mom, I center myself as defined by my role as their mother. Where is who I am in the mix of the roles I serve for others? I have a part of me that is independent of those roles, don't I? Social identity theorists say that "the core of an identity is the categorization of the self as an occupant of a role, and the incorporation, into the self, of the meanings and expectations associated with that role and its performance…. These expectations and meanings form a set of standards that guide behavior." I get that. Being a daughter comes with rules. There are also guiding principles for being a partner and being a parent.

Maybe it's my natural aversion to authority or my oppositional nature when people tell me what to do, but I'm struggling sorting through that set of standards. Who wrote that rule book anyway? Who set those standards? How do we decide if we are game for those rules or even write new ones if we don't know who the heck we are outside the rules that were set for us? Our role identities and our relationships are vital to the people we are. Got it. No doubt. But if the only way we know ourselves, or can define ourselves, is in relationship to others, without them, who are we? When our parents are no longer with us. When our relationship status changes. When our kids desert us to go off and live their own lives. Who are we left with?

I asked my dad once about his own identity, and he looked at me as if the question was immaterial and maybe a little indulgent. Since I am writing an entire collection of "indulgent" essays about my own identity, I pushed him and asked again. He remarked, "I don't have an identity. I have responsibilities." My father may only identify with his role identities and not be interested in unpacking or understanding the other layers of his identity. Maybe it's his age, his generation. Maybe it's his own authority issues coming out to play. It may certainly be from his upbringing; he is his father's son.

The level of responsibility placed on his father at a very young age was intense, and many of my grandfather's options were driven by those givens. There is no doubt my father absorbed the rules and guiding principles from his father and from the social environment he grew up in. He takes his role to support and provide for his family very seriously. That support extends to the small group of people who have been loyal and committed to that family as well. Not unlike a traditional Italian structure, family is the nucleus, elders are to be respected, and dads carry the weight of the earning.

Regardless of why my father isn't concerned with his own identity beyond his responsibilities, I find it fascinating. I am endlessly curious about the continuum of approaches to identity from my grandfather on one end, prioritizing only his role identity and my child on the other, deeply committed to allowing their personal identity to lead the way. I guess I'm somewhere in the middle, still trying to figure it out.

* * *

I'm proud of my dad. Part of my identification as my father's daughter is embedded in that pride. My dad has always been a huge influence on me as well as a haven. That mixed bag of respect and safety is embedded in my identifying as my father's daughter. In my experience as his daughter, I am protected; I am safe. I am where I need to be. No matter the moment, I am understood and accepted. There is never a crisis you cannot handle. All will be okay.

Over time, I have had to become more comfortable with ways I am not like my father. The more I disagree with him or see him as a human being and not as a figurehead, the less I associate with the label of being my father's daughter. This is a work in progress. It is hard to voice my opposition or fully accept the viewpoints or approaches we don't share. That doesn't mean I love him any less. It just means I know him better. I know myself better. I am not relying on my role as his daughter to be my default safety net. But I still come home to drink wine and talk about the meaning of life. I still come home to pick him up and make him go to music venues in the middle of the desert or whatever nutty thing I ask him to do, to which he most always says yes. I still come home for that mix of understanding and being told that everything will be okay.

There is nothing I am prouder of than being my kid's mom. It's certainly the coolest thing that's happened to me so far. It is a role I have happily allowed to consume much of my life. It has provided me purpose, a new perspective, and it has connected me to people in a way I hadn't imagined it would. It comes with me everywhere, feeds into conversations with almost everyone I interact with. It is a touchpoint, a common ground, a communal language. Parent to parent. This is as equally brilliant as it is, at times, boring. There is so much more to my life than only being a parent. I am more than a mom. All moms are more than their mom-ness. But the work of being a mom, or the primary caregiver, can be overwhelming and all-consuming. It takes over our thinking and our doing. It consumes our brains and bodies with topics and activities exclusive to the mom/child domain. We can easily remain isolated in mom groups and only talk to our mom friends about mom things. This perpetuates a cycle of sameness, reinforcing our mom role as all we are. We happily do it, but it takes a toll.

The other day a colleague who knows I like to travel said, "Oh, your kid is a senior? So they will be going off to college soon. That's great. You will get your days back, and you can travel anywhere you want!" What? Are you kidding me! Getting my days back sounds awful. And thinking about traveling anywhere I want without my favorite travel partner, my kid, just sucks. I'm terrified. I mentioned the conversation to one of my mom friends, who immediately gasped without me even needing to finish the story. She immediately understood my horror. Who am I without my role as a mom consuming my day-to-day? I don't really want to know. I'd like to ignore the question, but I need to know. Don't you?

There is safety and comfort in my role as my child's mom. There is safety and comfort in my role as my father's daughter. They both come with community and support that have made me who I am, but they are also somewhat stifling. It can be difficult to sit in that contradiction. There is also freedom in knowing I am more than those roles. More than my child's mom. More than my father's daughter. More than someone's something. We all are.

IN PRAISE OF CRYING: AN INSTAGRAM CAPTION

———

"I'm just so grateful, because to feel this vulnerable means I'm alive."

—BRENÉ BROWN, AMERICAN WRITER AND PROFESSOR

@mlombardidc[1] Hello My Instagram Family! I just wanted to check in to let you know that I am ok. Thank you to all who have DMed to check on my mental health. For those of you who have seen, commented on or shared the @buzzzfeed snap, which was super intrusive btw, I wanted to set the record straight, to let you know what actually happened and stop all the rumors. So here it goes. The other day I was sitting outside @starbucks and was crying. 😣 I did not have dust in my eyes. I was not laugh/crying at another viral meme. I wasn't

---

1. This is my actual IG handle, but the handles used in this chapter are not real people, I have made them up. They are not the real words of anyone; they are my own.

watching a virtual wedding or funeral. I was flat-out crying at my computer because I got hit with a wave of emotion due to living my life. That is what and all the pic captured.

@caringforyou25 are you sure you are ok?!!! 😩😣 #mentalhealthmatters

@mlombardidc Yes, I am ok. Just some everyday emotions filling up and overflowing. Totally normal thing to do.

@caringforyou25 ok but let me know if i can call someone for you i got you. your #mentalhealth is key

@mlombardidc TY I appreciate your concern but I'm feeling good. got good peeps around me if i need it.

@caringforyou25 ok. follow me and send me your number so you can get on my daily motivational messaging txt chain!

@yourhustleandgrinddude just get back on track. walk it off. keep the hustle and grind you will get there! 💪

@mlombardidc um not sure how that acknowledges my emotions but ok. not sure walking it off helps on this one dude.

@yourhustleandgrinddude you don't need to be a bitch about it 🤬 #realmendontcry

@mlombardidc wow! that was unnecessarily aggressive #realmenwomennonbinarytranshumansdocry

@mlombardidc I'd just like to add that crying gets a bad wrap, y'all. Can we just #normalize this for a second? Why do we need to avoid or suppress or judge it? You are not a stronger or weaker person because you do it. Your identity as a man or any gender for that matter is not undermined by doing it. How about we remove the gender stereotypes and shame filled self talk and let it go? crying is a universal exercise, experienced by everyone. it is gender, race, class, and age, neutral. We all do it. Just like everybody poops, everybody cries.[2]

@badassbosslady432 i'm here for it! I do it at home all the time. but there is no way I could cry at work

@mlombardidc OMG yes! I hate crying at work. I can feel the tears coming, I try to push them down which makes them come more, which makes me mad, which makes me cry. ARG!!!

@badassbosslady432 I'm the boss I'm supposed to be composed and look in charge.

@mlombardidc I get it. the stigma is real. but why do your tears make you less in charge? make you less capable of making good decisions for your company or leading your team?

@badassbosslady432 it doesn't. maybe we can start of movement to encourage crying at work

@mlombardidc yes! #badassbossladies #letthetearsfly

---

2. Taro Gomi is the author and illustrator of the classic 1979 children's book *Everyone Poops*. If you have not read it, please do! It is on the summer reading list for every newborn and their parent.

@badassbosslady432 ♥♥

@brenebrowne I love what you are saying! vulnerability is our super power as human beings and we shouldn't shy away from it. lean into it. make friends with it. make love to it.[3]

@mlombardidc @brenebrowne wow! can't believe you are following this thread. TY so much for your comment! the make love to your vulnerability is throwing me off a little bit... but i love the idea of vulnerability as a super power. Our vulnerability is something that makes us more powerful, special, unique, and visionary.

@comicbookobsessed123 I'm digging the whole superpower thing #batmanisrealandlivingindetroit but a lot of superheroes hide their identity due to their super powers. they are afraid of the risk living their truth will have on their family. Well Iron Man doesn't. also Luke Cage and the Fantastic Four are out but... anyway... I don't think we want our vulnerability, our emotionality, to lead us to hide who we are.

@mlombardidc ok super good point **@comicbook-obsessed123** maybe the metaphor breaks down a little there. we certainly don't want to hide our identity. the goal is to be out in the world as a vulnerable person who expresses their vulnerability in a variety of ways, one of them may be crying at their local Starbucks. 👻♀

---

3. As much as I would like to be Instagram buddies with Brené Brown, I am not. It would be super cool to have her comment on something I have posted. Alas, it has yet to have happened.

@comicbookobsessed123 or crying at the comic book convention after reading issue #121 of the Amazing Spider Man when Gwen Stacy died

@mlombardidc or that.

@comicbookobsessed123 😭😭😭😭

@mlombardidc so y'all, where is the last place you let tears fly? You clearly know my answer to this one. Tag me and let me know and use the hashtag #icrytoo. Love you!

I'D RATHER BE THE VERB THAN CREATE THE NOUN

"While we have the gift of life, it seems to me the only tragedy is to allow part of us to die—whether it is our spirit, our creativity or our glorious uniqueness."

—AMERICAN COMEDIAN GILDA RADNER

My dreams of becoming a YouTube star were dashed by my child. They have decided that we are not destined to be the next famous family band like the Osmonds, The Corrs, The Jackson 5, or even Hanson. We can MMMBop with the best of them, but alas, it is not to be.

For years—holidays, birthdays, Mother's Days—we have been recording videos for my mom. A little guitar, a lot of harmony, and quite a bit of banter come together to create our own version of a handmade gift for my mom. It is wonderful when you can create a gift for someone else when making it as much a gift for yourself. My child and I have always shared a love of music, as clear a family trait as any. Although I do or have played the piano, guitar, and harp, singing has always been my musical outlet of choice. From the back seat of the car, to children's choir, to opera, to musical theater, to cabaret clubs, to harmonizing with my kid, I have been singing in some form for most of my life. It was inevitable to pass that musical inclination down to my child.

I don't really know if creativity can be passed down, but it can certainly be modeled and absorbed. The data is a little wonky on this, but it's pretty cool that it is being studied. Even if my kid had not already been artistically inclined, they were doomed at the start. Their first few days in the world were a rush of tubes and tests and a lot of singing. While spending eleven days in the hospital after arriving six and a half weeks early, all I knew how to do was sing to my small little being. What else was I going to do? We certainly weren't going to have a logical conversation about how to manage the crisis of them leaving my Easy Bake Oven early. I really didn't want to think about that. I just wanted to sit with them and sing. So I did.

For some reason, after years of singing thousands of songs, the only three I could remember in my post-delivery state were the Arlen and Harburg classic "Over the Rainbow," "Blue Moon" by Rogers and Hart, and Ricky Nelson's "I Will Follow You." I couldn't remember the lyrics to the last one, so I made up new ones just for the two of us. Music became our first method of communication. It continues today, as we are always singing. I used to make them laugh by making up mini-operas about mundane things, like running errands, commenting on people walking by, or turning their favorite picture books into operettas and making up new melodies as I sang them night after night. We sing our lungs out on the hour-and-a-half ride home after picking them up from their dad's, kicking it off with some Broadway show tune, or anything off the soundtrack to *Stephen Universe*. Music has underscored my life, and like a good friend; it is there in the chaos and the calm.

After a choir performance early on in my child's musical journey, another parent and I were gushing about our brilliant kids, talking about our love of music, and he mentioned there was an adult choir I should join. My child demanded of me later that under no such circumstances was I allowed to join that choir because choir was their thing, not my thing anymore. There wasn't room for us both to sing in a choir. There have been multiple times when they have been possessive about the activity they are exploring, as if someone else joining might inhibit their discovery of whether it is their thing or not. There is a natural inclination as a child to want to define your own path and break away. It is even more vital, I can imagine, when that child shares similar passions with their mom. How do you know if the love you feel for something is truly your choice when you are surrounded by everyone else's love of the same thing? Love is contagious, which is why we need a heck of a lot more of it. But it can also be smothering when it doesn't allow room for others to breathe.

Creativity has always been an outlet for me to process my feelings, to channel them in some way. It made them manageable. It gave me control over them in a way I desperately needed. I could direct everything I was feeling into a song or a piano or a harp or a guitar. I could sing other people's words, interpret other people's stories, and see my worries or pain through them. It took the pressure off me to express those thoughts and feeling directly and allowed the music to do it for me.

When I was in college, I would hide in a practice room at the music school for hours, just banging out the accompaniment to a song until it felt right. I was impatient with my sight-reading skills, so I would make up my own arrangement based on the chord progressions listed above the staff. I'd repeat the song over and over, louder and louder, slightly different each time, just banging it out. Just me and the piano. In some ways, I felt she knew more about what I was feeling than I did. She could feel it through her keys and patiently let me abuse her so I could get it out of me.

I tried to write poetry, write songs or write in a diary, but it never fit. I hated the permanence of it. The thought of going back and reading my thoughts and feelings years later seemed intrusive. It defeated the purpose of what I was taught and what I believed: Never look back. Do things. Experience it. Feel. Then move on. My creative outlets in music allowed me to do that.

* * *

The journey to define ourselves is as much about determining who we are as it is understanding who we are not. It is interesting to me the identities we hold onto permanently and the ones that are just passing through. The ones that stick and the others that fall away or adapt. Being a creative has been stitched into who I am from day one. Throughout my life, one creative activity was added on or replaced by the other in an outpouring of exploration. In an effort to sustain harmony, my creative side ebbs and flows, seeking to match up with my pragmatism. A dance to keep the left and right brains in balance.

I am a creative. This I know myself to be. It has never confused me, but labeling it took some time to understand. There is something powerful about naming who we are. It makes it real. It takes it out of our mind, out of our body, and into the world. I have mostly resisted labels, seeing them as an effort to pin me to a box that I usually reject out of principle. Part of the reason this book exists is an effort to discover the language to define myself. Whether I actually use whatever language I discover remains to be seen. But being a creative makes sense to me. But I am not an artist.

The first time anyone asked me directly if I was an artist was in graduate school, and I didn't know what to say. I'd never thought about it, nor had it come up before. My artistic identity was taken for granted in the other spaces I inhabited. I felt a little panicked and insecure I hadn't thought about the answer to this pretty obvious question. Are you an artist? The professor who brought it up was doing that thing when someone asks a question that is really a statement, only leaving you room to agree with his question/statement and not actually answer it. This is quite annoying. His point to the small room of budding MFAs was that if you are here, if you are pursuing a master of fine arts, you are an artist. So name it. Announce it. The challenge was compelling but also laced with an all-too-familiar arrogance that comes from an older man telling a group of mostly younger women who they are and what they should do. But when I sifted through the pompousness, I had to acknowledge it was an important question to answer.

For me, the artist identity is like that dress I have in my closet that is stunning but just doesn't feel comfortable. It is tailored with exquisite stitching and looks fabulous on if I abstain from queso and too much chenin blanc. When I have worn it, those who recognize the designer would comment how good I look, but those who didn't were left out of the conversation entirely. It felt confining, like another thing I had to fit into. It just didn't feel like me. And besides, anything that limits my queso intake is a no-go.

I struggle with the confining nature of being an artist. Being an artist usually has a specific outcome attached to it. People can argue about how to define that outcome, the quality of it, but something must be created for it to be art. If I am an artist, then what I do is create the thing that is art. Being a creative, my outcome is indeterminate. The outcome of creativity is endless. Creativity is an act, an action, not an outcome. I would rather be the verb than create the noun. My creativity can show up anywhere it chooses and is wildly inclusive. My creativity is visible in the way I look at the world, how I problem-solve, as well as any projects I produce. It is holistic and encompasses the full person I am, not just the works I may create. It is a state of mind, an approach to being and working. It transcends industry and doesn't require me to produce in defined mediums.

It feels good to own being a creative. It is like a best friend that has been with me my entire life. Our relationship has grown and changed like the best relationships do—but I can count on it to be there for me always. It is exciting to imagine where it will lead me next. Wherever that is, they better have good queso.

CAN I PLEASE GET A DECENT BRA WITH MY FIREBALL SHOT?

"Fishing is boring, unless you catch an actual fish, and then it is disgusting."

—COMEDIAN DAVE BARRY

Seward is a small port town in Alaska. It is on a southern inlet that serves as a commercial fishing and tourism gateway. According to recent population statistics, this rustic town happens to be the 6,398th largest city in the United States, home to roughly 2,800 people. My boyfriend at the time and I were on a road trip around Alaska, exploring everything we could pack into eight days. Our main event in Seward was to hike up the Harding Icefield Trail and stand atop the ever-receding Exit Glacier. A most practical if uneventful naming, Exit Glacier was named such because it was where the first explorers exited the massive Harding Icefield. Exit Glacier sits a couple miles outside the little town of Seward. We had spent the day before in the Katmai National Park, thankful to the brown bears who were gracious enough to allow us to spy on them while they fished for salmon in the many rivers and streams fed by Brooks Falls.

I have done my fair share of fishing. Certainly not as adept as those brown bears, but I can hold my own. Every summer during my childhood, we would depart from Indiana and drive out west to meet our fishing grandparents and cousins for a little camping. It seems almost archaic to think that one could travel halfway across the country without a GPS or a cell phone. Armed with a blue Suburban, camping supplies, an atlas, and a CB radio, we could get anywhere we needed to go. My mom and aunt would agree on a location, a desired date, and off we went.

At some point, my brother and I labeled our grandparents by the activity that seemed most identified with them to our toddler minds. We had fishing grandparents whom, you guessed it, we did a ton of fishing with. We also had a set of airplane grandparents, who always arrived by airplane when coming to see us. The labeling provided a comfortable shortcut that made perfect sense for our little brains. When our parents would tell us we were going to see our grandparents, we would ask, "fishing or airplane?" This naming outlasted its necessity, but my brother and I cemented them into long-term nicknames. Our grandparents were certainly much more that than their fishing and airplane monikers, but the names stuck, and it didn't seem to bother anyone.

Associations are completely understandable; they help us remember how we have met someone or where our lives intersect with the person. My brother first met my friend Laura thirty years ago at a restaurant called the Crab House. For years later, whenever I would mention her, he would say, "Oh, Crab House Laura." I would confirm, yes, it was the same Laura he met at the Crab House. The problem was for years and years, every time I mentioned Laura, he would again say, "Oh, Crab House Laura." This is a woman whom he had seen and spent time with multiple times after that one Crab House meeting, a friend who plays an important role in my life, yet all he could do was ask me repeatedly, "Oh, Crab House Laura?" It only ended when I yelled at him. "I keep asking you to remove the Crab and the House from Laura's name! I need you to stop it now!" It required my anger to get it done.

When we lock in labels for people, we cement them to the defining characteristics or circumstances that created the label to begin with. Sometimes we are conscious of that choice, we do it on purpose, and other times we do not. I used to create superhero nicknames for the men I dated. There was Anger Man, Indecision Man, Army Man, The German, and Bondage Boy, to name a few. In speaking of myself in the third person, I was Practical Girl.

It started as a lighthearted way of coping with strong elements of my dudes' personalities: things I was coping with, trying to better understand, or that I found hysterical. I also used it to comment on inflection points in our relationship. Things I was trying to deal with. Anger Man jumped to anger quickly to manage his emotions. Indecision Man liked me but not commitment. Army Man wasn't actually interested in anything but himself and the Army, and I wasn't either of those things. The German was, well, German. Bondage Boy brought his control issues into all areas of our relationship.

In some ways, the nicknames shielded me from the emotional impact of the characteristic I was struggling with, and it also helped me navigate where I did or did not fit in with the things they put front and center. It was a way of exploring whether I belonged in this relationship with this man. I was longing to belong. Aren't we all? I wanted to find my place, my people, a relationship that would fit both of us. Either way, it locked me into seeing these men as their nicknames suggested. I was Crab House Laura-ing the men just like my brother had Crab Housed my friend Laura.

* * *

The night before our glacier hike, the Boat Man and I found ourselves at the local pub, where I was introduced to my first Fireball shot. Not one to say yes to anything in a one-and-a-half-ounce glass because of an unfortunate experience with Wild Turkey in my youth, I surprisingly said, "Sure, why not."

Now, I travel as often as I can. It is a form of inspiration and relief. Whenever I travel to a new place, I ask myself, "If I lived here, what would I do?" It gives me a framework for getting to know the environment. It allows my entrepreneurial brain a creative exercise. It provides comfort. Finding the answer requires me to get to know the place a little better than I might otherwise. To do this, I have to listen, watch, and ask questions. To go places that may be more local than tourist-oriented, I imagine and am curious about the environment that I'm in. I arrive with the knowledge I am an outsider.

I am often more comfortable as an outsider. It is safer, less vulnerable. When you want to belong, and you don't, it can be devastating. When I travel, there is no expectation of belonging. I am a temporary guest in a foreign country or in a new city. It relieves the pressure of belonging, which is welcome because, at a deep level, it is what I am most in search of—and what is the hardest to find. Always being aware of whether I fit in is exhausting. I want to fit in but am drawn toward those who stand out. I appreciate systems but am often questioning them if they are stupid. Back home, I am eager to belong but eventually, find myself the outsider in someone else's community. Trying to balance my desire to belong with my comfort as an outsider is a constant tug of war.

This exercise of imagining allows me to rehearse, without risk or consequence (aside from a potential hangover), what always feels like an inevitable next change. Solving the problem of *What would I do if I lived here?* calms my insecurities and proves to me that, wherever I land, I'll be standing up. It allows me to learn about new people, hear their stories, and, for a brief moment, remind myself I won't be alone when the next change arrives—a private insurance policy of sorts. Something that gives me comfort, quells any drifting I may feel. I wish I felt that just being on either side of that next inevitable change would be enough.

From the moment I said yes to that first great ball of fire, the evening unfolded into a low-key let's-get-drunk-with-the-locals bonanza, during which I learned a very important fact from the ladies at the bar: a decent bra was impossible to find in Seward. Maybe not all women locally felt this way, but my market research from the bar yielded unanimous results. No one sells a decent bra in Seward.

This nugget of information became the backbone of my brilliant (yet imaginary) newfound business opportunity in Seward. The female population makes up roughly a third of the town, and retail establishments skew decidedly toward their male clientele. At the time, Amazon wasn't an entirely reliable source for acquiring a brassiere in their remote location. In my inebriated state, I decided I would open up a nonprofit general store that provided a curated combination of products and mental health services for the female population in the area, bras included. It was an odd but admirable venture. I venture that my new temporary friends were on board for supporting. Thirty minutes into our hike up to the top of Exit Glacier the next morning, I was cursing all those one and a half ounces. I had to accept my new nonprofit might not be all that viable, but my brief connection with women in the bar was.

I'm trying to loosen my grip on questioning whether I belong or not and just enjoy being with the people I like to be with and those who want to be with me. It is starting to take the pressure off, with moderate levels of success. I've also stopped labeling my boyfriends, which I think is a step in the right direction. I've begun to think that whether I belong or not isn't as much about how others see me but how I see myself. If I label myself as an outsider, I am more than likely to be one. The labels we give ourselves are just as confining as the labels we give others. Maybe I don't need to be inside or outside. I just need to be present—with the men in my life, with the drunk women at the bar in Seward, and most importantly, with myself. And maybe I don't ever need to have a Fireball shot again.

HOW ~~NOT~~ TO PARENT A QUEER CHILD

———

"Parenting is the most important thing to many of us,
and so it's also the place we're most vulnerable. We're
all a little afraid we're doing it wrong."

—AUTHOR GLENNON DOYLE

I keep getting asked to write more about what it's like to
parent a queer child. I've resisted because I don't know the
answer. Yes, I am parenting a child who happens to be queer,
but I am not an expert in parenting queer children. My experience is just like all other parents who are parenting their
specific children—children who each have their individual
identities and personalities. My relationship with my child
isn't different because they are queer. We aren't unique or
special. We are amazing, but their queerness and my parenting of that queerness do not play into our awesomeness. It
is interesting how their T and Q in the LGBTQ+ landscape

somehow makes them a special case deserving of their own child-rearing manual. Parenting is universally difficult and rewarding no matter the circumstance, affinities, or identities. So I don't know how to write an essay about how to parent a queer child.

I struggle with books that are geared toward a specific gendered group of child-rearing. How to parent girls. How to parent boys. How to raise good daughters. How to raise strong sons. I recognize the majority of our children are sorted into boys and girls camps, and there is value to understanding the personal and societal pressures placed on each side—as well as the impact those pressures have on our kids and us parents. But I'm not eager to see books that overtly or inadvertently help parents keep our kids confined to those categories. I am much more interested in conversations that place our kids' genders as just one of many elements of their identity. An element that can ebb and flow like the rest of them. An element that is interesting and important but no more so than their kindness or creativity. I like books about how to raise children who are curious and think for themselves: how to raise children who will eat what I cook and do the laundry without being asked. Okay, well, maybe the last one is too specific to my current need. But I'm sure I'm not the only parent who would buy that book.

While I don't have a step-by-step guide for parenting queer children, I can share the following discoveries and insights from my experience as the parent of my beautifully unique kick-ass kid. Maybe they are like your own insights or discoveries. Maybe they are different. The only thing I know is they are true for me, and I imagine may ring true for some of you as well.

The Worries

I worry. As parents, we all worry. It is a universal experience that connects us all. Our worries come in all shapes and sizes. Are we doing enough—are we doing too much—are our kids smart enough—are they too cold or too hot—why are they not sleeping—the book says they need to be at X percentile, and they are not, shit, is something wrong—I forgot their lunch, I suck—do they fit in—do they have friends—do they have too many friends, is that why they didn't get an A—are they getting bullied—are they doing their homework—are they on their phone too much—if I take it away will they hate me—are they happy—how are they going to get into college with those grades—and the worries go on and on.

We all have worries as parents; many of them are universal, and others are specific to our individual experiences. I may not have experienced the worry of whether my child may get pulled over for driving while black. I may not have first-hand experience as a parent living in poverty worrying about how to feed their children. But knowing those stories and those parents, how can you not worry with them? The underlying experience of worrying for the health, safety, security, and happiness of our children connects us all. We are no different in our act of worrying.

I worry. My child is from a marginalized community, a community that is targeted based on some fucked-up view that there is a right and wrong way to be, and beings who color outside those lines are to be feared and bullied; they are in a position to be attacked for simply being there. So I worry. I worry because I can't control that. I can move us to a safer community, advocate for them at their school, and support the activities where they feel like they can show up as themselves. I can do whatever is necessary for them legally and medically to feel strong. But there is so little I control. I can't stop it when they are bumped at their locker as someone snarks, "What are you, a boy or a girl?" I don't see it when they are walking in places where people stare at them, and they feel unsafe. I'm not there when adults yell at them for going in the bathroom of their choice. If I am there when that happens, I can puff up like a mamma bear and tell that adult where they can go, but that doesn't actually help. I feel better, but it just further embarrasses my child. So, I worry. There is so much I don't understand about what it means to be in their body, in their mind, in their experience—as if me knowing those things would actually make them safer. It wouldn't.

When they identified as the gender they were assigned at birth, I had this false sense of security that I could pass on everything I know about how to live in the world as a woman. That my womanly knowledge and experience would be a shield to protect them from whatever came their way. I would teach them how to stand up to anyone who would diminish their femininity. I would teach them how to deal with the need to conform to the expectations of what being a woman is supposed to be while also developing your own individuality. How to navigate other women who hate you for being smart or attractive. How to pinpoint the men who just want your performance. And how to find the wonderful people who are not like the ones previously mentioned. They would be armed with my own personal feminist manifesto.

I would say to myself, "Look at all the wisdom I can provide this child! They will be strong and defiant. A child who will take on the world, armed with the knowledge of all women." But, alas, they thwarted my ego trip. They demand that I see them as a person and not as a category. To advise and parent based on the need of the human they are and not my expectations, not the expectations of an entire gender.

Shouldn't we all be parenting without all those previous expectations anyway? My experience is valuable. It is essential. But if I want to raise a child who sees people as they are, is open-minded and curious about the world, and interested in people who are not like them, shouldn't I model that behavior in how I parent? My feminist, girl power, women rule the world ethos is authentic to me. Hallelujah! But my child's job is to develop their own personal manifesto, not adopt mine.

So, I worry. I worry I haven't taught them enough. I worry that I don't know enough. I worry that I can't protect them.

The Wonder

My child is a wonder. I admire their strength and self-efficacy. They know things about who they are at a young age that it takes decades for others to ever question—as illustrated by this book. They know their limits and enforce boundaries in ways that are frustratingly enviable. It's possible they came out of the womb that way. Sometimes I catch myself thinking, *I want to be them when I grow up.* Am I supposed to be learning as much from my child as they learn from me? I thought the whole point was for me to be the teacher and them the student.

During the height of the pandemic and before the vaccine, they made very clear what they would and would not do. "Why would I go outside, there is a massive virus out there that is killing people. Talk to me when there is a vaccine."

They weren't interested in creating a pod with their friends or seeing family once cases went down. They didn't cave to my pressure to stick their head outside or take a walk in the evening. Aside from hopping into the car to travel between my house and their father's, they stayed indoors for a year. True to their word, as soon as they were vaccinated, they started to venture out slowly.

Boundaries are having a moment right now. Everyone and their mom seem to be posting about or teaching people how to establish and enforce their boundaries. The tactics are useful, but it's hard to build a protective barrier when you don't know what you are protecting. Knowing who you are, your values, needs, feelings, desires, and goals are step one to setting (and keeping) boundaries intact.

* * *

It is a wonder to me that one minute I can feel like the smartest person in the room, parent of the year, tapping into some super-parenting serum. The next, I feel like a fucking idiot. I bounce from extremes. I'd like to think I am one of the Williams sisters with a racket in her hand, whacking that ball back and forth, aiming it where it needs to go. But really, I'm the tennis ball, at the whim of some other external momentum. Sometimes making a point and other times soaring way out of bounds—and usually ending up with a headache. It's not that I thought parenting would be easy; it is that I didn't really think about what it would be like at all.

I never imagined what it would be like to be a parent. My ex-husband and I never really talked about it either. There are a lot of things we never talked about, unfortunately. I always assumed I'd be a parent because that's what you do when you are married. You have kids. You complete the family, carry on the legacy, whatever that means. I didn't think there was another option. I did want a child; it just never occurred to me all that it would entail. I knew the CliffsNotes version of what being a parent would require, but I didn't spend the time to read the full story. In some ways, I think it was better that way. Sometimes too much information, too much knowledge, gets in the way of experiencing something first-hand. And parenting is meant to be experienced. It's not something you learn. It is something you do. It's an action. A contact sport.

So, I wonder how we have made it this far, my child and I. I am amazed that the act of parenting can still fill me with wonder, surprise me, challenge me, inspire me, and encourage me—and that I can still learn as much from my child as they may learn from me.

The Wine

One of my mottos has always been to "earn your cocktail." I like a good cocktail. But the motto isn't about the alcohol. It is about the importance of earning your respite. When you are done for the day, what have you accomplished, what have you done to earn your moment of rest or celebration? The goal isn't to beat myself into the ground and then get drunk. The point is to remind myself to reflect on the day and toast it with a glass of wine or whatever suits your fancy.

In hindsight, it doesn't surprise me that I developed a more sophisticated taste for wine when my child was in pre-school. We skipped the terrible twos and made a beeline for the intolerable threes. A bit after that, my interest in wine began to develop. I knew what I liked and didn't like when I tasted it, but I didn't know what to ask for. So, I went to Steve, who owned the local wine store in town. I told him of my ignorance and that I wanted to learn, but I didn't know where to start. He asked me a couple of basic questions, and we developed a plan. He would sell me a bottle of wine, and when I came back, I had to tell him what I liked or did not like about it. Afterward, he would pick me another. He removed the pretension out of the process. I didn't have to use fancy wine words; I just described it however I liked. Sometimes, he would translate what I said into wine speak for fun, but he always suggested something that led me to learn more about what I liked and didn't.

Parenting gave me a whole new understanding about what it meant to earn that cocktail. I have never worked so hard or felt so spent. My bones, brain, tissues, and cells were exhausted from navigating everything that went along with life and parenting and working full time. What I thought was busy and challenging before paled in comparison. So, when the day ended, I popped that cork and poured a glass from the bottle Steve picked out for me. I had earned it. It occurs to me none of this is unique to parenting a queer child. It's universal to the whole parenting landscape. To moms especially.

The image of the wine mom has cemented its place in pop culture over the past ten or so years. In some ways, maybe I am one, a wine mom. I am a mom, and I like wine. "If you asked a self-identifying wine mom to explain who exactly the wine mom is, she'd likely tell you that she's a busy, exhausted parent who just needs a break and a laugh, a moment to remember who she is other than 'Mommy.'" The mom part of who we are is all-consuming, especially when our kids are young. It is easy to get lost in the matrix of mommy land. The other parts of who we are can get exiled to some outpost. The longer we stay away, the harder it is to find where we left those pieces of ourselves. It is inevitable that the priorities of our lives will ebb and flow. The responsibilities we have and the roles we play in the social environments we choose will jockey for some semblance of prominence over each other. But how do we not lose our personal identity in the process? How do we keep who we are intact? How do we make sure we aren't drowning that loss in wine?

In some ways, my single-parent life has helped me navigate that balance in unexpected ways, out of necessity. As a co-parent, 100 percent of my time is devoted to my kid's care when they are with me and when they are not, their father holds 100 percent of those same responsibilities. The traditional structure of mothers' duties and fathers' duties breaks down because each of us is responsible to just be their parent when they are with us. We don't argue over gender roles in parenting because it isn't relevant to our co-parenting relationship. Our needs and challenges are different.

Whether my child has been gone for a weekend, a week, or half the summer, I have been stuck, required to figure out something to do in their absence. When they were younger, that something to do was sleep, watch movies, decompress. But as time has passed and they have grown older, I've explored more of what it means to be me without them. I've engaged new activities, travel, friendships, and relationships independent of my role as a parent. I'm not suggesting single parenthood as an antidote to feeling overwhelmed by your parenting responsibilities or that everyone dump their partners in order to find themselves. My time to myself was structured because of divorce; maybe your time to yourself can be structured as well, just to less extreme measures. Take a couple of hours a week, a day, a weekend, a week, or half a summer to explore what else you enjoy. Allow yourself to yourself to be inspired by other things. It could be the start of something quite exciting.

* * *

I am encouraged that my kid already knows the difference between their personal identity and the mash-up other identities they are trying to figure out. Part of it is just who they are, and part of that is due to their queer identity. Their nonconformity is an advantage. They don't see it that way, but I do. It doesn't mean it isn't super hard and it won't continue to be difficult. They exist in a world that wants their conformity, to which they will not oblige. Hallelujah! Maybe that becomes part of their own personal manifesto. I certainly hope so.

ONE HUNDRED
HEART PILLOWS

———

"To love oneself is the beginning of a lifelong romance."
—PLAYWRIGHT AND POET OSCAR WILDE

Way back when my child was four, I hand-stitched them a small heart pillow for Valentine's Day. Little did I know that one small pillow would launch me on a four-year creative project that would ultimately help me through one of the most difficult periods of my life.

Their father and I were in the beginnings of a separation and subsequent divorce, and my child and I had recently moved into the home my parents were finishing building for their retirement. On February 14th of the year in question, I presented the original little pillow, made out of repurposing two shirts they had grown out of. My child was over the moon. Cuteness ensued. Hugs happened. All parties were happy. Project complete.

As you are well aware by now, I have always been a creative person, with creative outlets coming out of my ears. Creative activity was also a welcome part of life in our family. When I was young, my mother was often doing a variety of handcrafts; she drew maps and sketched. My brother and I had outlets in music. My dad, an academic, was passible with a reed instrument but more creative in the shop, always eager to tinker, build, or fix anything. Although music was always my first love, I also found handcrafts surprisingly satisfying. There were about nine months committed knitting scarfs. There was a time in the late nineties when I made nothing but beaded AIDS ribbons you could pin to your shirt, which I gave to everyone I could think of. I also made mosaics for a brief while, and the list goes on.

After my child's initial excitement over the gift subsided, the happy little monster asked if I could make them some more little heart pillows. *Sure, why not.* It didn't take me that long. "How many would you like?" I asked. "I want one hundred heart pillows," they announced. Finding it a funny request and not taking it seriously, I asked, "What are you going to do with one hundred heart pillows?" They countered, "I'm going to lie on the bed with all the pillows, and they will cover me with love." *Shit. Well, that was super cute, now I'm screwed, how do I say no to that?*

Maybe it was the guilt I felt from all the changes going on around them. Maybe I needed something to focus on to take my mind off the ensuing trauma. Maybe it was because I totally understood the desire to lie on a bed with one hundred heart pillows and be covered with love. So, I said yes.

Everything was changing around me, changing in ways I didn't quite understand. All I knew was I made a decision to leave. I couldn't anticipate all the things I would be leaving, all the changes to come. I couldn't anticipate how my life would be transformed, but I knew I needed to be out of the house I shared with my husband. The rest felt confusing and out of control. I was standing on the edge of something, and I really didn't know what I was doing. The only thing clear at the time was the four-year-old holding that little heart pillow. The only thing I knew for sure was that they were cute as hell, and I knew how to sew.

Because of the expected and unexpected interruptions of life, the project took me a couple years to complete. It became a creative project that kept my mind focused, my heart engaged, and ultimately brought order to the chaos. Most importantly, it included regular positive feedback from the little person I loved most in the world.

To get started, I needed rules. I wanted guidelines and governing principles. How the hell was I going to complete this project without an orderly plan? At a time in my life when I was at the mercy of lawyers and courts, nothing much felt in control. But I could make a damn pillow however I wanted; I could make one hundred of them if I wanted. It was nobody's business how I did it but mine. No one had to review it. No one would yell at me about it or question my mental state about it. No one would threaten anything having to do with it. It was entirely in my control. It was liberating.

My child seemed to be growing out of something once a week, all of which was moved from their closet to a bin in the basement to be sorted later. Colorful patterns, little phrases, and flamboyant ruffles all had turned this bin of discarded moments into something that suddenly had new purpose. It wasn't just clothes. There were old crib sheets and blankets and other textiles that had served their purpose but at some point became unnecessary. Had been forgotten. Once loved, kept close by but mostly ignored. I'd never really noticed how fun and joyful that bin looked.

One hundred heart pillows required at least two hundred pieces of fabric, and there was a treasure trove at my feet. That box birthed rule number one.

Rule Number One: A pillow can only be made out of fabric or materials that had once been utilized by my child. No fabric could be purchased for this project.

After making the first two pillows and running out of stuffing, I added an amendment to rule number one:

First Amendment to Rule Number One: I can buy filling to stuff the pillows, because you can't have a pillow that isn't stuffed.

It was easy in the beginning with all the fun and pretty fabric at my feet. I started with the obvious: the pretty patterns and bright colors. I flew through the first forty or so this way, each pillow taking about one or two evenings to complete. It was freeing. Just like when you start anything new; it's exciting, beautiful, and energizing. But as with most things, it got more complicated as it went along. After completing those first forty and working with the most obvious materials, I had to figure out what to do with the flawed fabric that was left. When I started looking closer, most of what was in the basement was flawed. The top layer may have been pristine but one layer beneath lay pieces honored with the stains and bruises that come from a lived experience.

As I stared at those imperfections, I wondered which ones could be incorporated or embellished—given new life, as it were. Which ones should be simply cut away? Some could be cut around and hidden in the fit of the pattern or the width of my stitching. But many were just too robust to be ignored. They were a part of the material now and had changed it forever, and maybe that is okay. The longer I stared at them, the more beautiful those bumps and bruises looked. A new opportunity emerged that led to a second amendment to rule number one.

Second Amendment to Rule Number One: I can embellish the fabric that had once been utilized by my child with items that had once been utilized by me. No embellishments may be purchased for this project.

There was a series of pillows made from an old crib sheet. The pattern, a modern interpretation of a botanical, was muted but still pretty. Small sections throughout were discolored from time and use. I unearthed an old box of beading supplies from my AIDS ribbon days and what seemed like another lifetime. Following the shape of the stains, I beaded over them, creating texture and sparkle for something that had been stretched, stepped, spilled, and spat on. The imperfections that led to the sheet being discarded inspired something new and beautiful instead. I had so much fun adapting the bruised crib sheet that I kept digging for the new challenge.

I configured one pillow from a shirt made entirely out of ruffles and buttons, in the end resembling a tuxedo shirt from the sixties. A couple pillows were made from a ribbon curtain that used to hang as the gateway into my child's room, which I wove in a checkered pattern before making it into a pillow. Each little pillow became a story in and of itself. It held the memories my child had with that item; at the same time, it held my hand through the challenging day to day. It kept me focused on little, meaningful accomplishments—little wins.

At some point around pillow sixty, my child started to lose their excitement over each new pillow. As I lost my positive reinforcement, it started to become clear the project wasn't actually about them. It had become a way for me to process my grief, to prove it was possible for the past not to define my future and the scars of a life lived are beautiful and can be reborn. This prolonged, repetitive, and simple act of creation had given me a gift, as had that box of old stuff.

It took about nine months to create seventy-five pillows, but the last twenty-five took much longer. I had already used everything I possibly could. I was waiting for my child to outgrow their clothes or lose interest in something I could make work. During that time, my life started to change, and new opportunities emerged. When I finally hit one hundred, there was no culminating moment of lying on the bed surrounded by one hundred heart pillows. Most of the pillows were back in the basement in my parents' home. Some had been given away to my nieces and friends' kids. My favorites had traveled with us to our new home four hundred miles away. The accomplishment was quiet but no less meaningful to me. My child smiled at the news and gave me a hug. They didn't believe me when I reminded them of what they said they would do with all those heart pillows. "There is no way I said that," they affirmed. I smiled. We sat on my bed, both reading, and I remember feeling already surrounded by all the love I needed.

YOU BRING THEM

———

"I am made and remade continually. Different people
draw different words from me."

                                        —AUTHOR, PLAYWRIGHT, AND LITERARY

CRITIC VIRGINIA WOOLF

Over ten years ago, I managed an African dance summer
program that connected under-resourced youth with some
of the best dance teachers in the industry. In my experience,
professional dancers are the hardest working, most resilient,
and committed creatives in the business. We flew in teachers from all over the country to work with these raw, passionate, and powerful young people. Marilyn was one of the
African dance teachers for the program, local to the area. I
didn't know her well, but I remember her with great fondness.
During the time I knew her, she was an anchor amid rough
waters. She was steady in the face of chaos (of which there
was much). She was calm and powerful, a combination of
supportive yet unsympathetic to excuses. Fierce.

Discombobulated at times, as one is in the middle of a divorce, I remember venting to her after a long day about how I didn't know how to manage all the moving parts of this life in chaos I was living. I was trying to navigate the day-to-day at the same time, imagining how I was going to accomplish everything I wanted to—how to do it all.

I was mid-rant when I said, "This is all so hard. How do I keep moving forward? What do I do when I move, and I don't live near my folks? What do I do with my child when I have to go to meetings and interviews, and I don't have any help?"

She let me go on for a bit and then looked at me with a mix of affection and that look of a much wiser person looking at you like you are stupid and said, "You bring them."

As I stared at her a bit confused, she slowed it down for me and said it again, "You bring them."

Marilyn cut through my noise in three little words, stating that at the end of the day, you've gotta do what you've gotta do to get what you've gotta get done. It isn't always going to fit neatly into the expectations set for you or even the expectations you set for yourself. But do it anyway. Unapologetically. If you need to bring your child to the meeting, you bring them. If you need to schedule your interviews around your life responsibilities, do that. You will disappoint people; they will disappoint you in their reaction to your choices. Expect it. Don't fight it. You can't twist yourself to fit a pattern not cut for you. Make a new pattern.

* * *

I have been bringing my child with me for as long as I can remember. To work and meetings. On vacation. To events. To the bar for football games (probably shouldn't admit that).

Wherever and whenever necessary or desired. It is second nature to bring them, I've probably become a little too comfortable with it—and I am unapologetic about it. Marilyn gave me a gift. She gave me permission to see my life, my options, in a new way.

But what happens now when my child is no longer there to bring? For thirteen years, it has been just us, our core family of two, with an extended family of many who love and care for us—but the day-to-day is just us. It has been liberating, challenging, exhausting, rewarding, and so much fun. It is complicated to sit with the contradiction of feelings swirling inside me. I'm super excited for what's next for them—college, young adult life—at the same time, I'm fighting the urge to lock them in their room, so they never leave me. I know logically that just because my nest is emptying doesn't mean I am losing my child. They are still here, alive and well, kickin' it, moving forward with their life preparing to face the next set of adventures. As am I. But emotionally, I feel like screaming, "Don't abandon me!"

Who am I without my child in my life every day? Without my days structured around their schedule? Without the daily, weekly, monthly shared milestones and experiences? Without Uno in front of the fire, or takeout night, or our travel adventures, or giving them hugs when shit gets real and them returning the favor? I've been by the side of this little person for the past seventeen years; it is strange to imagine my day-to-day without them. Who will I use as an excuse to get out of the things I don't want to do? You mean I have to be honest and admit that I don't want to attend? That doesn't sound right.

Discovering who we are is just as important as understanding who we are without. So much of who we are is channeled into the pillars that hold up our life: our parents, our partner, our kids, our job. Those parents, partners, kids, and jobs are like the stilts that turn a houseboat into a property on the shore. The reality is the house is still a house, safely on the water, with or without whatever is holding it up.

* * *

There is a picture I took of my child at four. It should be in an aspirational Capezio ad for children's dance attire. They are posed beautifully outside the dance studio door before their first ballet class: cherubic, staring up at the camera, hands clasped in front with a light smile, draped in the requisite pink tights and leotard. They had just spent the twenty minutes before the snap spinning in the dance studio lobby. This is the kind of image that would be added to the childhood photo montage detailing their rise to super dancer stardom as a finalist on the latest season of *So You Think You Can Dance*—the moment it all started. All this would be iconic if our child had not decided "no way," that ballet class was not for them once inside the dance studio. My child was sitting in a circle with a bunch of strange kids, all of them staring at this one adult, also a stranger. They started crying. They continued to turn up the volume on the tears until the dance teacher relented and escorted them out of the room. Their dance career was over before it began, but I still have the glorious picture.

My child has always known their own mind. Even if they didn't quite know how to express what they were feeling, they have always been able to find a way to indicate if something doesn't feel right or is not for them, whether you want it to be or not. Strong independence, anxiety, a little risk aversion, and a lot of logic combine to make it so.

For their first five years, they were terrified of the happy birthday song. Their father and I ruined the song the evening of their first birthday and luckily have the moment captured on video for us to peruse whenever we want a reminder of what early childhood trauma looks like. We were on a cross-country road trip celebrating their first birthday and stopping along the way to see friends. They were perched in a highchair with a slice of cake the size of their head in front of them. Their father and I, along with the two friends we were visiting, were standing beyond the cliched piece of cake. We all slowly start walking toward our poor child, smiling too broadly, singing too excitedly. I imagine them thinking, "Who are those terrifying clowns, what have they done with my parents, and who are those other two strangers moving toward me?" Their expression moved from confusion to discomfort to downright terror in the eight seconds it took to get the verse out.

Thanks to our terrifying display, during every subsequent birthday party until they were five, they would either cry, squirm away, or quietly disappear to avoid hearing the happy birthday song. They didn't need our permission. They just found the quickest way out of the room during the dreaded tune. They didn't care if their friends wanted them back or if we tried to convince them otherwise; when they were sure the song was done they would return, but not a moment sooner.

Moments like these have been repeated throughout their seventeen years: whenever they are confronted with something they don't jive with or doesn't feel right, they are out—independent of the peer pressure from parents or friends that surrounds the activity. They wouldn't ride the school bus when they were five and six because it didn't have seat belts, and as they stated, "You told me I have to wear my seatbelt in the car. The bus has no seat belts. That isn't safe." They were done with trick-or-treating at about nine years old after venturing out with a big group of friends. We were all walking down the street, turned the corner, and came upon a very lifelike window display of an animatronic butcher cutting off a mannequin's leg, accompanied with blood splatter and lighting effects to enhance the experience. They came. They saw. And they were done. They turned right around and started walking home. I stopped them to ask if they wanted to do something else. They said, "No, I'm done," and they kept on walking. Even now, they won't take an Uber because you aren't supposed to get in a car with a strange man. They say as soon as the car services allow them to request a woman, they will use it. It's hard to argue with their logic.

* * *

Sometimes permission can come in the form of three simple words like "You bring them." Sometimes it comes by example. Either way, it can provide you a different perspective, an alternative way forward when you feel stuck. The presence of another person can also give us permission to do the things we may have never thought of. Or not do things we would prefer to avoid. They provide us cover when we have a hard time making a choice on our own or admitting the choice is ours.

I am a closet introvert and yet have spent most of my career in social roles that require building events, teams, programs, and being out and about with the community. I love the work but am often exhausted because of the energy expended. I started blocking off time in my calendar to "Stare at the Wall," during which time, you guessed it, I stare at the wall to decompress. It can be hard to manage my love for engaging with people with the toll it takes on my mental and emotional energy.

Often, I have used my child as an excuse to get out of social activities I don't want to do. It allows me to avoid outing myself as tired or spent or just not interested in attending. They are my own little Captain America shield that makes me stronger and protects me from the barrage of social expectations and obligations. They have provided me cover and enabled me to lie. White as those lies may have been, they were still lies.

When you have the option, it can be easy to hide the part of yourself that feels out of sync with the circles you are living in. A kind of FOMO kicks in and taps you on the shoulder to say, "Hey, see all those extroverts over there, standing in front, shaking hands, jumping from event to event? Aren't you supposed to be doing that? Go do that. Why are you staring at a wall? What is wrong with you? Why don't you want to do that?" The truth of the matter is there is nothing wrong with me, aside from the little lies.

Often we can find excuses to avoid telling our truth and lie because it's easier than owning who we are and what we want. As comfortable as I am bringing my child with me, I now need to learn how to let them go, to leave them at home. Step out from behind the shield they provide and borrow a little of their uncompromising nature to just say no. I need to do the things that help me meet my goals, the activities that support the people I care for or make me feel good—only say yes to what aligns with my values and desires and honors my physical, mental, and emotional health. I'm lucky I have my child as a role model.

I'm doing all I can to prepare for this next stage of my life, the life where I only bring myself. I've written this book to help process my thoughts and feels. I've launched a whole new career, all in an effort to take control over my fear. But as much as I want all the work, building, and launching to save me from feeling the loss of the nest emptying out, it won't. The change is coming whether I'm ready for it or not. It is true the only constant is change, but the companion to that constant is pain. The more we try to stop change from happening or avoid the inevitable pain that comes with a life fully lived, the less full that life is. I've been thinking about the famous quote from feminist poet Edna St. Vincent Millay's letters, "Where you used to be, there is a hole in the world, which I find myself constantly walking around in the daytime, and falling in at night. I miss you like hell." My child is still here with me, but I can't help but miss them like hell already.

THIS SINGLE PARENT
HOME IS FAR
FROM BROKEN

———

"If the rules are not broken, we will be."

—YOKO ONO

I am a proud single parent.

My child does not come from a broken home. They have a home that is full of people who love and support them; there is so much love that it takes two houses to hold it all. They are not some product or statistic of a marriage that didn't work out. They are the outcome of the two people who had makeup sex after a fight that started during intermission at *Wicked* on Broadway. After fifteen years together, those two people got divorced. Our child was four years old.

* * *

My child and I sit cross-legged on my bed, looking at a flyer for a local LGBTQ youth choir and googling the terms listed on the page. The language to identify oneself within the LGBTQ world has expanded significantly since my youth, and I have no idea what some of these words mean. We are both pretty solid with gay and lesbian and bisexual. Shouldn't we all be by now? But sitting here, adding to an already eclectic search history, I am typing in a bunch of words with the prefixes of "pan" and "poly" and "a" and learning the difference between "curious" and "romantic" instead of "sexual" is a lot to decipher. This could be awkward, but we are actually having a blast, and thankfully, Grandma Google is here to help us out. Secretly, I am reveling in the fact that my child knows only a bit more than I do. "Hallelujah," I hum to myself quietly, as this is an unexpected victory.

I felt pretty secure in my parental superiority until my child was about three years old and started putting themself in time out. They would make a strategic decision whether the thing they wanted to do was worth the punishment. Seeing time-out as not much of a punishment but more a respite on the stairs, they went about doing what they wanted. When caught, they would walk themselves over, dramatically plop their butt on the bottom step and announce, "Mommy, I'm in time-out." At that early moment, I knew I was going to have to rethink the common misconception that I, the parent, was in charge.

Today we both agree I am a terrible disciplinarian. This is partly due to my natural lack of skill and because I gave up trying around that three-year mark. Our disciplinary conversations have been more about my child understanding the consequences of their actions and taking responsibility for them and not about my regulation of their behavior. If they didn't want to do their math homework, I was fine with that, but when asked by their math teacher why they didn't turn in that homework, they had to tell the truth—"I didn't do my homework because I didn't want to, because playing a video game or playing with the cat was more important." And the reality was owning up to that truth and disappointing their math teacher was enough of an imagined consequence to get their homework done. It was much more powerful and persuasive than the bottom step.

There are a lot of consequences that are already built into the actions we take, our own and our kids. I remember arguing with them for a week about why they needed to walk to school with a sweater while they refused to put it on. Exasperated, I finally stopped forcing the issue; after a couple of days, they accepted that it was damn cold outside without a sweater, and they never forgot outerwear again. Some of their learned accountability came from the circumstances of our lifestyle. I would have loved to be able to bring them the lunch we forgot or the book for class or their gym shorts, but it was just the two of us; I was at work, and it wasn't possible. They may have been pissed at me at the time, and I felt that all-too-familiar mommy guilt for not being at my child's beck and call, but the reality was what it was. They had to adapt, and they did. We both did.

My child has always worked on their own timeline. They are not concerned when the developmental data tells them they should crawl or walk, or whether you think they aren't moving fast enough. They will do what needs to be done in their own time. The day before they were born, their father and I had just toured the community hospital where they would make their grand entrance. I had already structured the day in my mind. They would venture out of my birthing canal and into the world egged on by a little grunting and a lot of profanity. Sister Hazel would provide the soundtrack for the slip and slide into our family doctor's hands, and that would be that: a monumental but uneventful birth. But our child had different plans. Just one day after our hospital tour, two days before we were supposed to start birthing classes, and six and a half weeks before they were scheduled to arrive, they decided it was time to enter the world. The only thing that remained from my imaginary staging of their birth was the grunting and profanity. The rest was a whole new world.

* * *

I never really imagined motherhood when I was younger, never really thought about marriage either. I'm not sure why. It seems like a rite of passage as a young woman, but for some reason, it wasn't a part of my experience. I wonder if boys ever think about it—what it would be like to be married, to imagine their wedding day. Some of them must. I'd love to see more of those stories instead of the ones that limit the interest in marriage and the rituals that surround it as only a woman's domain. Although I was surrounded by mothers and married people, marriage and motherhood weren't presented as aspirations; they were givens, maybe even expectations, but I didn't feel the pressure for those two accomplishments to define me.

My mom doesn't remember dreaming of getting married and having a family either. She expected it to happen but says she wasn't planning it ahead of time. From an early age, she wanted to be a doctor but discovered a strong allergic reaction to formaldehyde, which nipped that idea in the bud. Instead, she became a botanist. The gender divisions in our family were pretty traditional: Mom stayed home with my brother and me while my father worked. But it was always clear my parents were partners in life and business. As my father's profile rose, my mother's contribution was essential to his success.

I have no memory of chatting with my mother about these things—you know, the kind of things mothers and daughters talk about. She tells me I didn't have much time or patience whenever she wanted to impart motherly wisdom. Whatever she wanted to say had to be quick. She was ahead of her time, using no more than 280 characters, tweeting me life lessons on the fly. I don't remember any of this, but I don't doubt her recollection. I picture my younger self sliding in and out of conversations with my mother, avoiding the details and inadvertently perpetuating our distance. I had places to be and stuff to do, horses to ride, songs to sing, and instruments to play. My mother and I would have never sat on her bed looking up gender and sexuality terms in *Merriam-Webster.*

* * *

The narrative of a child from divorced parents coming from a broken home is a toxic one and prioritizes the influence of the institution of marriage over the influence of the people who choose to participate in the ritual or not. It reduces people, their experiences, and their stories to stereotypes. The marriage doesn't make a home broken or complete; the people do. And what does *broken* or *complete* really mean anyway? The whole theory around the broken home in America requires a common agreement that there is an ideal family structure, to begin with, one that includes a mother and a father: one female and one male. That ideal family is made possible by a marriage that sanctions the good ol' baby-making to complete the family. This feels like an absurd way to define what is ideal.

The history of the institution of marriage is fraught with inequities and power differentials that are certainly *not* ideal. That history has made the option of marriage limited to those who fit and exclusive to those who do not. Thankfully, this is changing, but there is still work to do whenever the power of the institution is more important than the needs of the people. A structure worth aspiring to is a home full of family, biological or chosen, that love each other, support each other, and behave in ways that align with that love and support. How that family structure is formalized, through a marriage or not, should be solely up to the individuals who want it. Or not.

I struggle with the concept of brokenness. I understand the common refrain that we are all broken, that we all come to the table with scars and wounds. As Hemingway stated, "The world breaks everyone and afterward many are strong at the broken places." Our lived experience requires those wounds, and our survival depends on it—it is in the fine print of the contract we sign upon birth. *Upon exiting the birth canal, you will enter a world that will provide you pain and ecstasy and every feeling in between. If you wish to avoid said feelings, you are shit out of luck. Please sign here _____.*

Hemingway's quote continues, "But those that will not break it kills. It kills the very good and the very gentle and the very brave impartially." If we are not willing to break, bend, scar, risk, love, and live, we die. So, a life well-lived is a life full of those scars, which seems pretty complete to me. That life doesn't seem broken at all.

I worry about the consequences of seeing ourselves as broken all the time. When I think of that brokenness, I can't help but picture it tethered to this destination labeled "fixed" on the other end. I don't want to be fixed. It feels like triage, like patching up the holes with a barrage of Band-Aids and then pushing me back out into the world stamped "new and improved." I would rather normalize our scars, talk about them openly when possible, and prioritize our mental health equally to our physical health. I'd like to experience all of this on a continuum, understanding that life is complicated and messy for all of us.

* * *

My child is three, and we are lying in the grass staring at the clouds. They are babbling about one thing or another as I listen. They talk a lot. Incessantly.

At times, I would ask them, "Hey, baby?"

"Yes, Mamma?"

"Why don't we practice silence for like thirty seconds or a minute, so we can experience what silence sounds like?" I tried to convince them in an overly cheery tone.

They giggle, "You're funny, Mommy."

For some strange reason, they thought I was joking. So, they just kept on talking.

But today, lying on my back next to them on the grass, I feel like I could listen to them go on for hours. I'm not sure I'm really *listening* to what they are saying, just enjoying the sound of their voice, feeling their energy and excitement. Everything is new to them. I forget what that feels like. What it feels like to learn a new word, see a new thing, or discover a new taste. My senses have dulled. But right now, I'm content just being beside them, soaking in their wonder. I'm still. At peace. I don't feel the need to prove anything in this moment, only to give them 100 percent of my time and attention.

My connection with my child makes sense to me. It isn't something I need to convince myself of, or explain, or justify to others. It has no self-talk attached to it. It just is, and it is beautiful. I belong. It is the only place I know I belong without question. It centers me. It is surprising. I have spent a lot of time in my life changing and adapting. Moving forward. Running. My child gave me the gift of teaching me how to stop, to stand still. I like this feeling. I love it. Belonging is intoxicating. I ~~want~~ need more of it.

It was amazing what happened when I simply stood still. All sorts of feelings and thoughts and wants and needs started flooding toward me. It was hard to know what to do with it all, but at the core, I knew I wanted more of *that* feeling. The feeling of lying in the grass with my child or singing to them at the hospital. The feeling of walking with my grandfather. I wanted more. As I looked for that feeling, I mostly found its absence.

There was this strange simultaneous gaining and losing of agency I felt when becoming a mother. My time, my body, and my attention were now at the whim of this little creature. They had needs and wants that required me to respond in order for them to survive, needs that didn't take into account my to-do list. At the same time, I developed an innate ability to streamline the things that were in my control. My thoughts, my priorities, and my future plans all became much clearer. It was as if the filter I previously possessed was upgraded to a new model with all the bells and whistles. This new version filtered out the distractions, dumped the bullshit, presorted the stuff I actually had to address and presented it to me color-coded for my final approval.

There are times in our life when we have to ask ourselves: Are we who we want to be? Are we living *our* life or making choices fed by the expectations of others? Are we following a path we have set for ourselves? Have we even stopped for a moment to think about the choices we are making? I asked myself, and I didn't know the answer. Once the wheels start rolling, it can be hard to slow down enough to hear the questions, let alone discover the answers. I remember standing with my dad, ready to walk down the aisle to get married, music playing, our guests waiting in anticipation. I turned to him, and I asked, "What am I doing?" He looked at me, very directly, clasped my hand tighter, and said, "You are getting married. That is what you are doing."

I wanted to get married. I'm thrilled I did. I don't regret a thing. But I didn't really take the time to think about what I was doing. My best friend in the world asked. I loved him. That is what you do. You get married. I didn't know any different. I didn't even stop to ask if there were questions I should be asking. After the proposal in front of our families, my future hubby and I went outside to escape. He was frustrated because his mom had pulled him aside earlier to ask if he really wanted to propose, to get married. He found that annoying; we both did. Of course, we wanted to. Of course, *we* wanted to get married! In hindsight, I think back to that question, and she was the only one who thought to ask. To inquire. What we found insulting at the time was actually a highly reasonable question as I look back.[4]

Our marriage broke down. The routine wear and tear wore it out, the marriage failed to function, and we couldn't fix it. In hindsight, I wish we had spent more time lying in the grass looking at clouds and asking each other questions—who knows what we would have learned if we had.

---

4. I am a huge fan of my ex-mother-in-law. We exchange texts now and then, and I see her on very rare occasions, but I like her tremendously. During and post-marriage I spent very little time with her alone. But the times I did, I always wished I had done more of it.

* * *

I have been a part of the marriage club, the divorce club, and the single parent club. All of them welcomed me with open arms. Yet, I found over time that connections based only on my membership to some club rarely led to lasting relationships. My married friends found it awkward when we split. All of the previous couples' activities I had been invited to stopped. Those married friends found it too uncomfortable to navigate, and we clearly weren't good enough friends to begin with to make it through the choppy waters. I gained a whole new group of single-parent friends that suddenly appeared as my status changed. I'm not sure if I had finally noticed them or they were more eager to get to know me because of my new circumstances. But I was now suddenly welcomed into a whole new community.

It is inevitable and desirable to develop relationships with people based on circumstances, environment, or ideology. We have school friends, work colleagues, extracurricular- or community-based connections—nothing wrong with that. Some deep friendships can develop that way; it happens all the time. But when our circumstances change or ideology adjusts—when we break away, if we haven't made deeper connections, our belonging to that group ends.

In some ways, becoming a single parent was a change like any of the others I had experienced; it required another disruption and then an adaptation. All the previous moves I had experienced—moving towns, houses, schools, and jobs—included shedding and then regrowth. If you are good at change, which I am, there is something comforting about knowing a new adventure is always a change away. But this change wasn't like any other. The tapestry that was my relationship with my ex-husband, my best friend, my marriage, had a tight weave—threading it took time and attention, and untangling it required the same.

As my unraveling tapestry continued to pick up steam, I started to notice how my shifting membership impacted how I saw myself and how others saw me. Every other transition I had experienced didn't seem to have the same kind of destabilizing effect. What I had imagined as a two-dimensional impact—between the triad of myself, my child, and their father—became four-dimensional, impacting elements and individuals I wasn't expecting. Friendships disappeared, family relationships changed, and community connections shifted. I was standing with my feet in the sand as the tide rushed in and out, trying to figure out how to make the sand stop moving.

Our pathways are established by our family, school, community, and society. All of them structure lanes for us to follow. In many ways, this can be helpful for those who easily fit in or are empowered and thrive in the opportunities provided. But for those who don't or choose to opt-out, it can range from inspiring to challenging to downright unsafe. A change that is empowering for one person can feel threatening to another.

Professor Rosabeth Moss Kanter explains, "Change interferes with autonomy and can make people feel that they've lost control over their territory. Our sense of self-determination is often the first things to go when faced with a potential change coming from someone else.... If change feels like walking off a cliff blindfolded, then people will reject it." There is no doubt I lost control over many things because of my divorce, and I certainly walked off a cliff, but the territory sometimes seemed to include people who need not be affected. Our choices have ripple effects on other people. This is expected for the folks who are close to us, but sometimes our choices or our stories are inflated to impact people we don't actually impact directly.

My marriage, divorce, and single parenting experience is unique to me. It is unlike any other, not because I am so special but because I am me. My marriage doesn't magically allow me to know everything about every other marriage.

My identity as a single parent is not a slight on the institution of marriage or all the people who strongly identify with their marriage. My identity as a mother doesn't have anything to do with the others who choose a different path. My child's identity as trans/non-binary doesn't say anything about another parent's child. One identity does not negate or make permissible the other. My identity as a single parent doesn't distill the parenting options to single or married, of which you have to choose one. My child's trans identity doesn't impede the cis identity; it just adds another beautiful child to the landscape of children in this world. As the modern-day prophet Depeche Mode said so simply, "People are people."

We are comparative instead of cooperative. How are the lives we want to lead, or the identities we choose, a disservice to the life another may want to lead? How do we allow room for both, for more, to turn the "other" into another? How do we break the binary and move beyond the either-or? I'm not sure rules are meant to be broken, but it is inevitable that they will be. The things that confine us have a way of pushing us to break free.

WHEN AN OMANI MAN ASKS YOU TO GO BACK TO HIS CAMEL FARM, HE ACTUALLY WANTS YOU TO MEET HIS CAMELS

"Show a people over and over again as one thing and that is what they become... the single story creates stereotypes and the problem with stereotypes is not that they are untrue but that they are incomplete."
—AUTHOR CHIMAMANDA NGOZI ADICHIE

My child and I are standing in the lobby of a nice hotel twenty minutes from downtown Muscat, Oman. We are waiting for our guide, Omar, to pick us up and take us through the Grand Mosque. Upon arriving, Omar introduced himself and, after a couple pleasantries, gave us a debrief on what to expect upon entering the structure. Built seventeen years before our visit, the Grand Mosque is one of the most popular sites in Oman. It is a glorious cultural and religious site that feels otherworldly. It isn't old, but it feels ancestral. As a visitor, it was crowded, but I never felt confined. It was opulent and strangely minimalist at the same time. We were thrilled to visit.

There is something about religious buildings that have always attracted me. Although baptized, my brother and I were not raised in a religious faith. Yet everywhere I travel, I have to find the local place of worship, go inside if I can, walk the perimeter, and then just sit in silence. When I was younger, I used to wonder what it must be like to believe, to belong based on that belief, envious of the ready-made community attached to a congregation of faith. Although my faith has developed over the years as an amalgam of multiple belief systems, it still lacks that congregation.

Back in the lobby during our debrief, Omar confirmed I had my head covering, and I mentioned that my child had one as well. He quickly corrected me that my son would not need one. Recognizing this might not be the appropriate moment to explain the full scope of my child's gender identity, I simply corrected him that my child was female. He seemed confused and looked back and forth at my child and me, trying to reconcile what he was seeing with what I was saying. My child presents more masculine, identifies as non-binary, and was assigned female at birth. A couple inches shorter than me at five feet, six inches with a lean physique, they stood there attired conservatively in a long-sleeved button-up and light khakis, capped with a mop of brown hair betraying their youth.

As a guest in a majority Muslim country, with a passport that identifies them as female, we had an agreement before launching this adventure. Whenever necessary, to avoid conflict, we would strictly default to the gender they were assigned at birth and illustrated on all legal documents. After an awkward couple of moments, Omar finally looked back at me and said, "He won't need it." For punctuation, my child quickly tossed the headscarf back at me. I'm not sure if Omar understood or if all that really mattered in this moment was what appeared to be. And since neither my explanation nor Omar's observation was the truth, I let it go.

For the rest of our adventure in Oman, my child passed as a boy without complication. Aside from one very uncomfortable bathroom incident, the adventure was a wild ride of experiences and interactions wrapped in the more comfortable narrative of a mother traveling with her son. I'm not sure I would have noticed the difference if we hadn't spent the previous year's annual trip traveling around Morocco more clearly identifiable as a mother alone traveling with her daughter. Without a male companion, our experience in Morocco was considerably different than it was in Oman. Many voiced their concern for my missing husband.

Was he dead? We were stared at almost everywhere we went unchaperoned. Did we get separated from him? I was also propositioned multiple times. Yes, maybe he is dead? She will need a new man! I'm not sure if the Moroccan men felt sorry for my lack of a male companion or if they were looking for an opportunity to move to America, as one young man explained quite explicitly.

When I was planning our adventure to Oman, one big question I had to decide was whether to get a driver or if I would drive. We had a driver for the second half of our trip around Morocco, which was fantastic. Thinking about navigating all the twists and turns between Marrakech and Tangiers, even in hindsight, gives me hives. But we also felt trapped by having a driver, by our itinerary, by being stuck in the car without the option to get out and explore until we arrived at our predetermined destination. For a couple weeks, I explored all our options. I read blogs about women traveling solo around the country, collected insights, opinions, and practical travel tips, adding them into a document to help make the decision. Against the advice of my mother and encouraged by many female travel bloggers, I chose to drive and booked a little gray four-by-four. We were ready to roll.

It's possible it took me an embarrassingly long time to figure out how to start our little SUV when picking it up at the Muscat airport. Once we left the capital city of Muscat, aside from the loud beeping that screamed at me whenever I exceeded the appropriate speed limit, we were free to explore the beautiful and arid country. Our route resembled the Big Dipper constellation, albeit upside down. We drove from Muscat up into the Al Hajar Mountains, then back down en route to Sur with a short little drive back to Muscat. We had the water and the mountains. The sand and the sea. The city and mountain towns. The country was very easy to traverse; roads and petrol stations were clearly marked, and not too many people were on the roads. After spending a couple days in the mountains, we had some time to kill while en route to Sur, almost near the tip of where the Gulf of Oman intersects with the Arabian Sea. Looking for a desert excursion, we ventured off to find the Wahabi sand dunes a young Omani man at our hotel had suggested we explore.

It is relevant to know I have a terrible sense of direction. I always know where I am trying to get to, but I may not know exactly where I am or how to get there. The upside to this trait is I am very rarely bothered by getting lost and have enjoyed many adventures because of my detours. As a directionally challenged individual, I have developed a comfortable relationship with not taking the direct route to get where I want to go and have discovered sometimes where I wanted to go was not nearly as interesting as where I ended up. I have no problem asking for help when necessary and have met some wonderful people that way.

This is not a trait I share with my child. They hate to get lost! They don't go anywhere they are not clear how to get to. The destination has been mapped and practiced in their head before ever venturing out. They also have a better natural sense of direction than I do and are not interested in asking for help. They are suspect of strangers, especially strange men. I do not argue this point with them—it's a good instinct—but occasionally, my ability to make strangers friends bumps up against their desire not to.

En route to the Wahabi sand dunes, we stopped at a petrol station for a little gas and guidance. Post-gas and pre-guidance, the woman behind the counter and I entered into a delightfully intimate conversation about how much my son must look like my husband since he didn't look anything like me. There wasn't any point in correcting the "husband" part, and we had accepted the "son" part days ago; neither were essential to the conversation we were having. She asked me about my cultural heritage and that of my husband to decipher the nuances she was seeing in my child's face that were lacking in mine.

This was fascinating and kind of exciting because it was the complete opposite of what we have heard our entire lives. Most everyone agrees my child, and I look remarkably alike.

We could have been siblings if you look at pictures of us at the same age. Even as we have aged, we are still often greeted with the statement, "Well, you two are clearly related, aren't you?" I love that my child and I look alike and love hearing it reinforced by others. It feels good and powerful, and our shared features are a visible reflection of my own belonging to someone I love so deeply. Just their existence is the accomplishment that I am most comfortable and at peace with. It fills me with joy, pride, and confidence. It is simple. Uncomplicated. Just love.

The woman behind the counter gave us some general directions to the sand dunes, which I half-understood, and we went on our way. When planning a new trip, a huge part of the fun for me is the research. I love reading, looking up stories, learning about the history and cultural narrative of the environment, the industry, the people. I read travel stories from bloggers, often perspectives from female travelers, traveling alone or in small groups with other women. Looking for perspectives from people who may have a similar travel aesthetic or experience. Multiple times I came across the comment from female travel writers that went something like this, "When an Omani man asks you to come back to his camel farm for coffee, it is not a euphemism. It is a very straightforward request."

I am always conscious of being a woman traveling alone. I have traveled with a lot of different people over the years: family, husband, partners, best friend, my child, and alone. It's different traveling alone. I'm certainly not alone when I am traveling with my kid, but all the safety is still my sole responsibility, just like when I am traveling by myself. You get used to it, unfortunately. Thinking about protecting yourself. What to do, where to go when, how to behave, and whom to believe. When I was planning our trip to Morocco, my mom was extra worried about our safety, strange men, and the potential for danger. I remember reminding her what it is like being a woman in America, and many of the things she was worried about were just as possible right here at home. Unfortunately, in America, not everyone believes a woman's body is 100 percent her own. Thinking about safety is a given no matter where I am.

At some point after leaving the petrol station, I noticed a small pickup truck riding my bumper. Not sure where I was going and a bit annoyed by the wedgie the little Nissan was giving me, I pulled over to let him pass. He pulled up beside us with a cheerful greeting and asked us where we were going. I mentioned looking for a place to explore the sand dunes; I was already a little confused as we were surrounded by sand dunes and didn't understand where to go.

We launched into conversation. He spoke quickly and loudly through our rolled-down windows. All I understood was he was a guide for the dunes, he could help us, he had a camel farm, and he asked us to follow him back for coffee. The whole conversation happened in less than two minutes. It was fast and warm and awkward and confusing, and after I said, "Sure, why not," all I could think was, *What the hell are you doing following a strange man back to his camel farm?* But I kept reminding myself (absurdly) that everything I read indicated this was going to be okay. We were not going to end up on a *Dateline* special about the hundreds of women and their children who have vanished after visiting camel farms.

I had no idea where his farm was; he was leading, and I was following. I was not in control. As the dirt roads turned to sand, he stopped in the middle of the road. I followed suit. He got out of his car, opened my car door, pointed to the four-wheel drive, reached in and engaged it, got back in his car, and on we went. The flat sand path reached upward, then turned and continued upward some more. As we turned, he accelerated to prepare for the hill. It continued. Turn and accelerate into the hill. Turn and accelerate into the next hill that awaits. It was a blast, intimidating and thrilling all at the same time.

My child, risk-averse as they are, was staring at me as I drove. Without speaking a word, I could see the expression on their face as if their thoughts were screaming at me, "I'm supposed to trust you, I do, but you are testing everything I know about what is supposed to be going on right now? Mom, Mom, Mom—are you listening to me? Should I grab the wheel and stop you or let this play out? Oh, wait—is that a baby camel?" About seven minutes later, we were pulling up to the Omani man's camel farm. We parked, stepped away from our little four-by-four, and he introduced us to his momma and baby camel.

After meeting his camel family, he asked if my son and I wanted to go ride the dunes. He pointed to his car. He could tell we weren't thrilled about getting into his car, so he said we could take ours since it had four-wheel drive. He hopped into the driver's seat and motioned for my son to ride beside him. I was confined to the back seat. My brother and I spent a fair amount of time during the long summers of our youth riding ATVs with the cousins on their farm in Oregon. This would be similar, right? Not so much. He took off!

We climbed the sand, shifting gears as he fishtailed, spitting grains in the air. My child was frozen with a huge grin on their face. Their right hand was on the passenger door window, left foot bracing themselves on the floorboard, and left hand on the dash. Our new friend asked the young man sitting next to him if he knew how to drive.

My child said, "No."

"How old are you?" he continued.

"Fourteen."

Shocked and maybe a little disappointed in me, it must be due to my lack of a husband, I imagined him thinking. He said, "You must learn to drive."

At that point, while accelerating up a dune, he grabbed my child, pulled them half on his lap, foot on the peddle, hands on the wheel, and directed them what to do and when to do it. They accelerated, braked, and turned. Spin and repeat. He directed and encouraged, and they listened. It was a blur of words and smiles. Sand was flying, eyes were wide, and tension was high. All I could do was watch and wonder and want to hear the acerbic yet childlike interior monologue in free flow in my kid's head. "No no no—shit. Did he just…? Yes. What is happening. OMG! Mom help me. Are we going to die? Am I going to kill us? What am I doing? This is nuts. This is amazing. I'm the shit. I'm terrified. Yeet! I'm four-wheeling. I'm awesome. I have to pee. Stop. Whee!"

By the time we returned to his farm, our new friend had found a new pal in my son. He wrapped his arm around him, patted his back, seemingly proud of providing this right of passage—his first driving lesson. Spectacular as it was, it didn't occur to me until we had made it to Sur how unique this experience was for them, and how different it might have been had their gender been assumed as something other than a son.

* * *

Whether consciously or not, there is an expectation about what one does or does not do based on their gender, from how boys and girls are supposed to behave to what they get away with. What toys are provided. What sports or activities are offered. How girls and boys should look and what they should wear. What role they should play in their social relationships. Our gender socialization also teaches us what is the appropriate way to express (or not express) our emotions, and where and with whom we feel safe.

Gender-based decisions and expectations come from all sides: family, community, and society. When you are talking about doctors, scientists, or people in positions of power, what are the automatic pronouns you use? It's not surprising if it is most likely "he." Keep an eye out for it; it says a lot about our innate expectations. I still catch myself in that loop every now and then. Trans activist Thomas Page McBee wrote, "Most of us experience gender conditioning so young—research shows it begins in infancy—that we misunderstand the relationship between nature and nurture, culture and biology, fitting in and being oneself."

My ex-husband and I started buying boys' clothing long before our child had any interest in questioning their gender identity: baggy pants with big elastic waistbands, and wide T-shirts bathed in primary colors, dinosaurs, and trucks. What they lacked in style diversity, they more than made up for in comfort. According to the fast fashion options, it seemed that six-year-old girls only wore skinny jeans, leggings, and T-shirts with shelf bras in them. Not sure why a six-year-old girl needs a shelf for their undeveloped breasts and clothing that calls attention to any specific part of their body. It is inevitable that how we see ourselves will be influenced by outside sources, but the media and fast fashion industries hold way too much of the market share.

We can choose to divert from the established binary of gendered clothes, toys, and activities, but doing so indicates a deviation from the norm. There may be consequences for that, from family, friends, or the community at large. If we can just loosen our grip on our expectations of how our children express themselves, maybe we can open up the options for what they can experience. Why does it matter that much to us anyway? What does it say about us to have our child color outside the lines of our expectations? Whose childhood is it? It shouldn't be ours—that childhood is past due.

I don't suggest we live in a genderless world, that we don't buy our daughters dolls and our boys trucks. What I do hope for is we have more dolls that resemble the kids out in the world. More dolls that are multiethnic, different shapes and sizes, more non-binary and trans dolls. Barbie driving a monster truck and GI Joe playing dress-up. Just let kids do whatever the heck they want to with their toys, with their clothes, and with their hair. Allow our kids to express themselves however they choose. Allow their self-confidence and self-efficacy to develop and grow. Allow them to choose their life. Just loosen our grip.

My kid would like the world to see them as they are, and if it doesn't, fuck it. I can't argue with that. I would like the world to see me as I am, and if it doesn't... Please don't dislike me too much because that feels shitty, and I'm a little insecure about it. I look confident as fuck, but the reality is I'm just like everyone else who worries and struggles with vulnerability.

WHY CAN'T I HAVE A LESBIAN LOVER AS ATTENTIVE AS THE WOMAN IN 6B?

———

"The evils that now and then wring a groan from my heart—lie in position—not that I am a *single* woman and likely to remain a *single* woman—but because I am a *lonely* woman and likely to be *lonely*. But it cannot be helped, and therefore *imperatively must be borne*—and borne, too, with as few words about it as may be."

—AUTHOR CHARLOTTE BRONTË

Why can't I have a lesbian lover as attentive as the woman in 6B? Well, it would help if I were a lesbian, which I am not. However, if I were, it might have changed the state of my social life for the better post-divorce, living in the hills of western Massachusetts.

During my custody battle, I was commuting to Washington, DC, every week for work. During one of those flights, I experienced the worst turbulence of my life, descending from twenty-five thousand feet into Hartford from the Baltimore/Washington International Airport. I hate to fly. No, seriously, I really hate to fly. I love the experience flying allows me to have once I get where I'm going, but as soon as some brilliant Gen Alpha figures out teleporting, I'm all in.

You know it is going to be a nasty descent when one of two things happens. First, the captain seats the flight attendants and informs the passengers that it is going to get a little bumpy in his most "I am going to speak extra calm as to not alarm any of you passengers prone to panic" voice. Second, the loud, chatty passengers behind you who won't shut up about their son's hockey prowess finally quiet the motor in their mouths mid-sentence. Once it started, no petit four filled with lorazepam could have saved the out-of-control toboggan ride of a descent.

Sitting across from me was a couple in 6A and 6B. The turbulence began. Stoic, 6A clung to her seat, frozen, quietly tearing up. Ten years her junior, 6A calmly held her hand and spoke gently about what they had for lunch and where they were going to dinner when they got home. Every sentence or two, 6A would mumble a word: "Okay" or "mm-hmm" and "yes." It's a mundane topic, to be sure, but a simple conversation that seemed to help guide her partner through the really rough ride.

Without reprieve, the yucky descent took a solid fifteen minutes. During that time, I was well aware of my solitary state in that single seat, 6C. Back on solid ground and still a little shaky, my mother patiently let me vent about the flight as I waited for a jump in economy parking lot three twenty minutes later.

I can remember having such a difficult time distinguishing between being alone and loneliness around the time of that flight. I was so jealous that 6A had found someone who knew just the right thing to say to help calm her down. Little did 6B know, but being the proverbial fly on their wall while we all hurtled to what could possibly be our doom helped me too. My usual tactic on trippy flights is to sing to myself. After a short, intense bout of turbulence on a more recent flight, the woman in front of me looked through the seats when things calmed down and complimented me on my voice. Recognizing my surprise, she said, "It's alright, honey, we all gotta do what we gotta to get through it," and turned back around.

She is right—we all gotta do what we gotta to get through. We gotta be who we are. Sing "Over the Rainbow" loudly if it calms us down. Life is beautiful but it is also laced with some really crappy flights now and then. And if your partner talking about food gets you through, I'm all for it. I think we should all be aspiring to have a lesbian lover in our life like the woman in 6B.

* * *

Why does it seem that I am always surrounded by couples? They are everywhere. They seem to populate like rabbits, popping up all over the place. I can't go anywhere without seeing them at dinner, at the bar, at Target, in ads for pretty much everything. Hell, the hashtag #couplesgoals has 5.1 million posts. I recognize that I am probably just noticing it more because I am not coupled or married. It's most likely an illusion, an amalgam of one bias that notices the things I am looking for and another bias that confirms what I see as true. But if you look at the scientific research journal that is Instagram, #singlesgoals only has about five hundred posts, so it must be true.[5]

Marriages skyrocketed at the end of WWII, but since then, thanks to data from the National Center on Health Statistics, data on marriages has been riding a wave that gets lower and lower, hitting an all-time low in 2018. Interestingly, over the past ten years, as the marriage rates declined, so has the divorce rate. I want to assume it's a good sign that we are making better choices about whether to get married and with whom. According to a recent Pew Research Center study on single adults, half of them are not looking for a relationship; they have more important priorities right now. Men seem to be more eager to find a mate, while women are digging their uncoupled state. Damn straight! So, if the landscape of marriage, couples, and single life is changing, why do I still feel like an outsider as the uncoupled one? Maybe it's my age or my social circles (or my own insecurity), but I wonder where all those single people are? Maybe they really are all on Match or Bumble or HER or Lex looking to couple up.[6]

---

5. Instagram hashtags certainly are not a scientific resource. All the hashtag notations in here were provided via a quick hashtag search on Instagram. But social media has enormous power over our mental and emotional health. And if we are FOMO-ing hard over the fact that everyone's life and relationships look perfect on social media, it just perpetuates that fact that the single world is missing out on that perfection. There is a good amount of research on the mental health impacts of social media. Check this out: (https://www.ncbi.nlm.nih.gov/pmc/articles/PMC7364393/)

6. I spent a little time looking up queer dating sites. I know the cis-friendly ones quite well because of personal experience—maybe that's another book someday—but it was interesting reading more about dating from the queer perspective. HER calls itself the "biggest dating app for LGBTQ+ women and queer folk" (weareher.com) while Lex states it is "… text-centered social app that connects queer lovers and friends." (thisislex.app/)

Or maybe what is being reflected out in the world doesn't reflect what the data says. I want to see the uncoupled living their life out in the open. I want #singleandhappy to have 5.2 million posts instead of seventy-two thousand on Instagram. The real truth is I want us to stop measuring ourselves and each other by our relationship status.

Famous developmental psychologist Erik Erikson and inventor of the phrase "identity crisis," stated the somewhat obvious observation, "Life doesn't make any sense without interdependence. We need each other, and the sooner we learn that, the better for us all." Being socially connected has "been baked into our operating system for tens of millions of years." With family as the epicenter of our social connections, it makes sense that as we age, at some point, we start looking to establish the building blocks of our own family. I'm not mad at that. It's the pressure that bothers me. I'm as guilty of it as the next person. I joke with my child that at some point, they have to provide me with a grandchild; they don't have to be the one to birth that child—however it happens, it is up to them and their partner. But they have to get it done. That's a pretty standard and incredibly selfish request from the parent to the child. Not only am I expecting them to have a partner, but I also require that partner to pop out a kid for my benefit.

As a parent, we feel like we are owed a child for having one in the first place. That's terrible. Just as bad is continuing to pressure our children about their romantic relationships: Who are they dating? Do they have a partner? When are they getting married? And if you have siblings who are coupled up, it gets even worse. How come you don't bring anyone home for Thanksgiving like your sister does? My answer would be because there is too much damn pressure!

My parents seem to think it's funny, or not surprising, that I haven't found a long-term partner since my divorce. I'm too picky (according to my dad), and I should probably settle with someone at some point (according to my mom), so I am not alone. I try to ignore them both, but it makes me sad that I feel like I can't talk to them about the subject. I am not eager to bring anyone home because if it doesn't work out, there I am again, too picky and not settling to avoid dying alone.

And, hell, I have the same conversation with myself. *What is wrong with me? Why didn't that relationship work? Why is this relationship not what I want?* The reality is nothing. There is nothing wrong with me. There is nothing wrong with you if you haven't found the right partner yet. There is nothing wrong with you if you're not interested in dating, if you are focusing on other passions, or are aromantic. Look at me using Grandma Google's help there. Nothing is wrong with you. *Nothing is wrong with you, Maryann.*

We don't have ownership over other people's choices, and we shouldn't, no matter how much we want to. My own desire to have a long-term partner is for me to pursue. My dream to be a grandparent is a narrative for my future that I love. But it is entirely selfish, and I need to let it be. I can hope that they experience the love, purpose, and empowerment that parenting them has provided me. But my child's purpose in life is not to validate my own choices. It is to live their own.

* * *

It is Saturday night, and I'm home after another flight. I've got a glass of wine in hand, quietly celebrating my feet on the ground. I think back to 6A and 6B, and I smile. Right now, I'm by myself but I don't feel alone. Being alone is not innately tied to loneliness. You can spend years in the same room with someone and feel completely alone. And I can write at the dining room table alone and feel quite full. I look forward to a time when the seat next to me is occupied by a heterosexual male attending the flight with me, holding my hand while I sing show tunes during turbulence, but until then, I know I can survive it alone… and I always have the lorazepam for backup.

YOU LOOK GOOD FOR YOUR AGE: A VERY SHORT ONE-ACT PLAY

———

"I know not age nor weariness nor defeat."

—ROSE KENNEDY

Playwright's Note:

The year is some time pre- or post-pandemic or in a different reality in which the pandemic never happened. The time period is totally up to the production team. The subject matter is universal to a relatively recent American experience, but location and specific year is indeterminate and probably not that relevant.

The scenes should be set with minimal furniture that does not indicate any specific location or time period. Any realism of the locations should be illustrated through the lighting, projections, and/or sound design.

* * *

SCENE ONE

MARYANN is seated in the American Express Centurion Lounge at LAX with a couple hours to kill before her flight home. She has been talking to a cute middle-aged business executive, JONATHAN. She likes him. He likes her. There is a connection, she thinks. He's been pleasant, attentive, and a good listener. They have been talking for the past forty minutes, killing time before their flights. Convo has been easy, fun, and witty. Flirty. Did I mention he is cute? Yes. A good-looking man. Looks a bit like a clean-cut Jeffrey Dean Morgan, the dad in Supernatural, *but with maybe twenty-five pounds on him. She likes a guy with a little meat, so she's not mad at it. He is taking his time in the bathroom, though.... Hopefully, he's not calling his wife.... that would really put a damper on the conversation. Anyway... her mind is wandering... it is still a couple hours before her flight home.*

JONATHAN: *(Lightly excited. Speaks as he sits back down.)* Hey, sorry 'bout that, just got a call from the buyer I was telling you about. Looks like they wanna buy the house.

MARYANN: That's great! Congratulations. That must be a relief.

JONATHAN: You know it! My dad would hate it that I'm selling it, but I really don't know what else to do. It's not like my sis or I are ever going to move to Oskaloosa. *(They both smile.)*

MARYANN: *(Feigning fandom for the small Iowa city)* I'm sure there are lovely things about the town, someone wants to live there, they bought the house?

JONATHAN: That may be true… but not quite my idea of the "next great adventure." *(They smile at each other. An inside joke. There is totally a connection. A pause. The little banter has run its course.)*

MARYANN: *(She can't help herself.)* Are you married?

JONATHAN: *(Laughs a little at the bluntness but loving this next line of questioning)* No, I am not. Are you?

MARYANN: No, I am not.

JONATHAN: Okay, I guess we got that out of the way. You feel better that I wasn't on the phone with my wife?

MARYANN: Yes, I do. Thanks for clearing that up. *(They both smile. They freeze. Lights go down on JONATHAN. A seamless transition into Scene Two.)*

* * *

SCENE TWO

MARYANN turns in her chair as the lights come up to reveal SAM. SAM is full of energy, the same age or older than MARYANN, with a youthful aura around them. Their movements are fluid, and they have a hard time sitting still, but it's not distracting. MARYANN sees SAM, stands excitedly, and meets SAM downstage. They both wait to be seated as they talk.

SAM: So you know that kid in my office who does the branding for that new VR start-up?

MARYANN: Yeah, I think so.

SAM: *(Sounding a little bummed)* She just got called.

MARYANN: Oh, no! You liked her. That just sucks.

SAM: I know! She is so smart and creative and now... well, you know. She's just out. She would have been such a great addition to the fifty over fifty.

VOICEOVER: (It sounds like a man shouting outside the café. He keeps repeating the following, "You too could be one of the 50 million over fifty who survive. Follow @50over50 to avoid being nominated." At some point, someone goes out to move him along—he is disrupting the guests. Indistinguishable conversation ensues, then fades out.)

SAM and MARYANN move to their table as if being ushered by a host.

MARYANN: How's she doing? Have you talked to her? Did she ask you for an exemption?

SAM: No. But I spoke to her. I think she's okay. You know these young people, their faces in their phones. Facebook's propaganda machine did its job, and they think it's some kind of honor. They are all FOMOing over it with the other thirty under thirties posting these glossy congratulations posts. Like they "made it" or won the lotto. What the hell, people just eat it up.

MARYANN: I still think it sucks. I get it. I know how we got here, but it still sucks.

SAM: Not sure why grouping by qualifications or skill and expertise....

MARYANN.... or even desire. Like, do you *want* to go...?

SAM: Right! Not sure why all that stuff didn't get more votes.

MARYANN: People are just so obsessed with age.

SAM: They all just love their thirty under thirty lists. That's for sure.

MARYANN: True. I'm just happy I'm over fifty. That's all I've got to say.

SAM: Truth! No one is freezing my old ass and sending me off to colonize another planet because we fucked this one up.

MARYANN: Halle-fucking-lujah! *(They both freeze. Lights go down on SAM. A seamless transition into Scene Three.)*

* * *

SCENE THREE

MARYANN stands up and walks back to the chair where JONATHAN is seated, still frozen. Lights fade back up as she sits. There is an awkward pause. They are trying to figure out where to go with the conversation next...

JONATHAN: So...

MARYANN: So...

JONATHAN: Okay, I wanna ask you a question, but I don't want to be rude.

MARYANN: *(A little suspect of what is coming next)* Well, I'd prefer you not to be rude as well, but let's see what happens.

JONATHAN: *(A slightly longer than necessary pause)* How old are you?

MARYANN: *(Relieved)* Ha! I thought you were going to ask me my income or my medical history or why the hell I wore these shitty ass shoes today....

JONATHAN: I like those shoes!

MARYANN: Me too, but they are super uncomfortable.

JONATHAN: *(Teasing)* Well, that was a stupid decision when you woke up this morning.

MARYANN: *(In on the joke)* I know! Never again…. *(They smile. They are doing a lot of smiling…. It's cute but a little annoying.)*

JONATHAN: *(She still hasn't answered the question, just smiling.)* It's a sensitive question for folks. Not everyone wants to disclose. Not trying to pressure you. I just like you. Lots of feelings and division around the whole thing, with the thirty under thirties and the forties… I get it… I know it can get super politicized….

MARYANN: *(Interrupting him slightly)* I'm fifty.

JONATHAN: *(Super relieved)* Thank God! *(They both freeze. Lights go down on both of them. A seamless transition into Scene Four.)*

* * *

SCENE FOUR

Lights fade up on SAM, who is sitting at the cafe table alone. MARYANN has either left or is in the restroom. The WAITER has been walking by the table a couple times, keeping an eye on SAM, and finally comes over. SAM is getting a little annoyed by the attention.

WAITER: So, do you need anything? Anything else look good to you?

SAM: *(It's possible the waiter is talking about himself. Is this his attempt at flirting? Eww.)* Nope, I'm still good. Just gonna sit here a bit longer. Thank you.

WAITER: Okay. 'Cause it's not that busy and can get you whatever you need. *(He lingers.)*

SAM: Hey, if you need me to head out, I'm happy to get the check and wait outside.

WAITER: No! Feel free to stay.

SAM: *(Yeah, he's definitely trying to flirt. Not into it.)* Okay, sounds good.

WAITER: So, how do you two know each other? Your friend who was here.

SAM: Been friends for a long time, man. Hey, can you go grab me another napkin?

WAITER: *(Pulls a napkin out of his pocket and hands it to SAM. Feeling encouraged, he sits.)* That's cool. Just didn't know if you two were an item.

SAM: *(Not having it and not in the mood)* Wow. Dude, I think we can stop right here, and can I get the check?

WAITER: What! Hey, can't fault a guy for trying. You're beautiful, and you only live once, and who knows when we're gonna get called.

SAM: *(sympathetic to the "getting called" thing)* Okay. I appreciate the compliment; I really wish you the best. I won't be getting called but would really like the check now.

WAITER: What? *(getting it)* You're over fifty? No, shit! Wow, you look good for your age. Nicely done!

SAM: No. No. Not nicely done. *(Sam stands. They are not having this conversation with him.)* No. I do not look good for my age. I just look good. This is what a person in their fifties looks like, okay?

WAITER: Yeah, okay. It's just a compliment

SAM: *(Pissed at the "compliment" word, SAM looks across the cafe and sees a striking woman with long silver hair and calls out to her.)* Ma'am. Hi. Yes, you with the peach jacket and silver hair. Pardon me for the question, but how old are you? (*SAM is drawing attention from the cafe.*)

VOICEOVER: (*An older-sounding woman in her sixties*) Um, hi. I'm sixty-three.

SAM: (*To the woman*) Thank you. (*To WAITER*) See that beautiful woman over there? She is sixty-three. She is what sixty-three looks like. She is beautiful and striking and sixty-three. Take a look. Are you looking?

WAITER: Yes, I'm…

SAM: (*Interrupting him, SAM is getting on a roll and sees a young person staring at the scene unfolding. SAM tries to get the young person's attention*) Hey. Hi. How ya doing? Sorry if I'm making a scene. Just trying to make a point here. But do you mind telling me your age?

VOICEOVER: (*A young person in their early twenties*) Yeah, no worries. This kinda slaps. I'm digging it. I'm twenty-one.

SAM: (*Smiles back at the young person*) See that twenty-one-year-old right there? That is what twenty-one looks like right here, right now. They don't look old or young for twenty-one. There is no need to add a qualifier in order to reconcile the difference between what your perception of what twenty-one looks like with the actual twenty-one-year-old in front of you.

WAITER: I get it…

SAM: No. And just in case you don't get it: your telling me I look good for my age is NOT a compliment. It is an insult. (*MARYANN comes back from taking a call while this rant is wrapping up.*) The only thing your "compliment" does is remind me that in your youth-obsessed way that I have passed the expiration date of beauty and therefore have surprised you. I look this good over fifty. So just stop. (*Commotion can be heard in the cafe, people laughing, cheering, muttering. SAM tosses too much cash on the table, and SAM and MARYANN start to walk out.)*

MARYANN: What the hell did you start?

SAM: Wasn't my fault. *(They laugh.)* So, was that the airport guy?

MARYANN: Yes! His name is Jonathan. He's flying in this weekend. I don't know. Kinda like him. We shall see.

SAM: That's all you can do. He's over fifty, right?

MARYANN: Of course! No, seriously, what was all that about? *(they walk out arm in arm, chatting and laughing.)*

END OF PLAY

OH, CRAP, I JUST SHOULD ALL OVER MYSELF

"I always wanted to be somebody, but now I realize I should have been more specific."

—ACTOR AND COMEDIAN LILY TOMLIN

I slapped my brother in the face one time. I don't know why I did it. Well, that isn't true. I know exactly why I did it. I slapped him because I wanted to feel what it felt like. I was curious. I was also an idiot and thirteen. Objectively, I *should not* have done that. Both hindsight and foresight could have determined the no-go nature of that choice. My brother's "What the fuck?" expression confirmed the absurdity of the moment that had just taken place. If he had done something specific to piss me off, delivered me late to the barn to ride, or insulted my best friend's choice in music (The Beatles, by the way,) or had just run over the cat, then maybe his expression might have read "What the fuck? Wait, okay, maybe I get how that happened…" But no rhyme or reason was there to make sense of my idiotic action.

"Should" is a simple but powerful word. It is used to point out an obligation or a correct (or incorrect) course of action. That you should or should not do something. I should not have slapped my brother. I should get to work on time. My kid should turn in their homework in order to get credit for the work. I should not eat a whole pan of rice crispy treats because I know they will make make me throw up, no matter how yummy they taste.

A "should" is also a criticism at its core. In a passive form, it is innocuous and a moderately useful way of reflecting on our past choices. Maybe I shouldn't have used a fake ID to get into that bar at eighteen and then thrown up in the back of my car when my sober friend drove me home. In hindsight, the "should" frames the conversation and allows a moment to balance choice with outcome and put a checkmark in the appropriate column.

   _ YES, let's do that, or something resembling that, again.
   X NO fucking way am I doing that again.

But "should" is also problematic. Whether spoken out loud or delivered in silence, it can be wielded as a weapon of obligation from one to another. It is even worse when delivered from one to oneself. Its use indicates there is an appropriate way to behave, a right way to be. The meaning of the word "shall" and its past tense "should" are drowning in debt, obligation, and guilt. The use of the word comes with a root that is meant to confine and constrain, which is objectively terrible. Most often, we use the word to judge ourselves and others about how we look, how we behave, the way we live, and who we become.

* * *

I wake up as a woman every day. This I don't question. I am powerful and comfortable in my skin as that woman, and how I show up isn't up for questioning. The woman I am is nonnegotiable. How comfortable other people are with how I show up is interesting to me sometimes, as it says less about me and everything about the person who is uncomfortable—but their discomfort isn't a reason to rethink the woman I am. My confidence in that non-negotiability has developed over time. When I was younger, I spent a good amount of time trying to navigate between who I thought that woman should be and the woman others expected me to be. It took a while to solve the equation that led me to the woman I wanted to be.

The woman I am and the woman others expect me to be is the woman I want to be... No.

I spent a decade as a theater producer in New York City after I graduated from college. The first time I rented a significant theater for a show, the manager quoted me the price, looked me up and down, glanced back at his newspaper, and said, "You can't afford that." It's not like I hadn't been underestimated before or been told no when I wanted to do something. But this was the first time I can remember feeling so clearly my denial was based entirely on his perception of me, what I looked like, specifically my gender and my youth. It was not that I had never been judged based on what I looked like. I grew up as a girl in America with access to other humans and media and entertainment. Of course, I'd been judged. I was also in the theater; that is par for the course. But there was no purpose for his judgment beyond some preconceived notion that girls don't rent theaters and that I should not have the financial means to do so. I did have the means, though. So, I rented the damn theater.

> *The woman I am minus the woman others expect me to be is the woman I want to be... Not that either.*

I don't remember being parented in any overtly gendered way or being told by my parents or expected to do certain things because I was a girl. I also had examples where the gender rules, even when explicit, weren't always followed. When I was fourteen, I played the role of Amahl in *Amahl and the Night Visitors*, an opera by Italian composer Gian Carlo Menotti. Opera has a long history of remixing gender onstage. Some of that can be traced to the ban on women singing in church, so men and boys had to sing the higher parts. For a time, young boys were castrated to maintain their high voices. Throughout opera's history, women also dressed as men for "trouser roles," and the cross-dressing was returned when men dressed as women as well. Much of this was to maintain the vocal diversity necessary for the performance, not as a statement for gender equality. Menotti makes explicit in the production notes that "it is the express wish of the composer that the role of Amahl should always be performed by a boy. Neither the musical nor the dramatic concept of the opera permits the substitution of a woman costumed as a child." But I was cast anyway, which was an incredible experience.

The woman I am plus time and experience is woman I want to be... Yeah, that works better.

There is a long history of women and non-cisgender men being "should" on from all sides—from men, society (men), culture (mostly men), and media and entertainment (men and women) but also from other women. For some reason, the hierarchy (as it was originally developed) of who one should be, should look like, should act, and whom one should please requires some kind of maintenance. And we are still being "should" on in ways that should be unacceptable.

For many, there is a constant negotiation between who they are and the way others expect or demand them to be. That constant negotiation can impact their access to basic services, rights, education, and opportunities. This need to colonize another's experience in the name of anything—religion, politics, morals, family, or the ways things were done—continues to perpetuate a narrative that there is a right way to be and a wrong way to be. This binary view leaves little room for all the beauty and magic and inspiration that is in between and all around. Why are we so afraid of letting people be themselves?

* * *

While exploring the Mutrah Souq, a traditional Arab market in Oman, my child and I needed to use the bathroom. Let's accept that public restrooms are not high on the list of desirable establishments to visit in any country. When I was on that hiking trip around the Italian Alps, I was fascinated by all the unique signs on the men's and women's restrooms. Everywhere I went, I took pictures of the different images that directed travelers into the appropriate stall. All of them were strange and often funny icons of what a woman or man might look like and what costumes they would wear. We accept public restrooms as a necessary evil. Aside from a very opulent restroom I shared a moment with in Bloomingdale's in New York City, we usually get in and out of them as fast as we can.

Restrooms slapped with a "Men" sign on them are the least desirable of the bunch. I know many men, if given the choice, who would rather attend the women's room or a gender-neutral one to avoid the abstract art of bodily fluid on display in many potty stops for dudes only.

Back in Oman, this single-stall restroom welcomed me first as my child waited outside. As my child was about to enter the restroom I had just stepped out of, an Omani women yelled, "No," and proceeded to point to the men's bathroom. Fueled by the considerable language barrier, what happened next was an absurd back-and-forth between the woman and me as I tried to explain that my child, who may have looked like a boy, was a girl, who actually wasn't a girl, but we had decided it was easier and safer to stick to the gender on their passport, who most importantly needed to use the bathroom. I worked through every word I could think of; girl, woman, lady, female, before I finally became a mime making swoopy hourglass shapes with my hands and pointing to my child. Finally, the Omani woman understood, covered her mouth, apologized, then loudly started telling all the women around her that my child was a girl and pointing as they finally went into the bathroom. The whole incident was a mix of hysterical and horrifying and one that can't be completely dismissed by cultural barriers.

This was not the first or last time my child's choice of restroom was questioned by men and women, boys and girls alike, all of them "should-ing" on my child based simply on where they are going to relieve themselves. Can you imagine what it must feel like to a child to have an adult (of any gender) yell aggressively across the parking lot that they are going in the wrong restroom? It's terrible. How is that action anything but an adult bullying a child? How is that acceptable to anyone?

Professor and social neuroscientist Matthew D. Lieberman writes, "Bullying hurts so much not because one individual is rejecting us but because we tend to believe that the bully speaks for others—that if we are being singled out by the bully, then we are probably unliked and unwanted by most. Otherwise, why would all those others watch the bully tease us rather than stepping in to help support us. Absence of support is taken as a sign of mass rejection." Those rejections and bulling have ripple effects long after any one incident, leading to higher rates of depression and suicide. Is that really what we want?

* * *

These preconceived notions that others have for us, those beliefs that we should or should not be, do, or have access to something, have a lasting effect on how we feel. What others tell us is absorbed into what we tell ourselves.

I have a vivid memory of the moment my child realized that just because someone says they are your friend doesn't mean they behave like a friend. Crying in the back of the car, they were trying to reconcile what they thought a friend would be like, how having a friend would make them feel, with the reality that *this friend* treated them like shit. This friend kept telling them what kind of person they should be, what activities they should like, and looking down on them when they didn't agree. My child kept repeating over and over, "But she's my friend…." until it finally sunk in— she really wasn't. It was heartbreaking. Hallelujah, my child broke up with this friend soon after, proving you are never too young to learn how to set a boundary.

Boundary setting can be a bitch, but we all have to do it. We must set them to limit our time with unsupportive people. We must also set boundaries with ourselves and the voice in our head "should-ing" all over us. Hopefully, that inner voice is providing motivation, self-love, positive affirmation, and wisdom—helping to prop you up when you need it most. But that voice could also be comparison shopping yourself on behalf of all the "should" others people and systems have put in your path. I should be thinner. I should make more money. I should go to more PTA meetings. I should work harder. I should be more (or less) ambitious. I should just accept this dude; he's nice enough. I shouldn't have done this. I should have done that.

We all know the image of the devil and the angel sitting on our shoulders, pushing us toward good or bad outcomes. But that image is not complex enough. It doesn't quite capture how insidious the inner voice can be. It's important to treat her "should-ing" the same way we treat a toxic friend. Just because she is a part of you doesn't mean you need to give her any more respect than you would anyone else yelling at you about which bathroom you should use or telling you whom you should or should not love. What you should wear. How you should find it flattering to have men comment about how they like your ass. Would you say the nasty stuff you say to yourself to another person? Would you stand by and let someone say that nasty stuff to someone you love?

_ YES, I'd do that, or something resembling that.

X NO fucking way am I doing that.

It's time to let go of all the "should-ing." The "should-ing" we put ourselves through and the "should-ing" we shove on others. It's time to just let it be and shut the "should-ing" up.

WHAT'S A REAL JOB, ANYWAY?

———

"In order to be irreplaceable, one must always be different."

—COCO CHANEL

I was grabbing my daily, overpriced beverage from the corporate coffee shop that I wish I didn't love but do, and I overheard this woman on the phone. Let's call her Carol. Carol was venting her frustration about how her college-aged child just wanted to do musical theater, and that was not going to get her a real job. I stood there quietly eavesdropping, wanting to introduce myself as a musical theater degree holding person who also has a real job. But I didn't. This whole "real job" versus the perceived "fake job" bugs the snot out of me.

What is a real job anyway? Earning an income is necessary to support the lives we wish to build. That job can serve as a paycheck or can be your passion or anything in between.

You get to decide. All choices are valid. There is no right way to construct our lives or our careers. There is no real or fake, just what you choose to do—what feels right. Hopefully, that is in a place that welcomes you and treats you with the respect you deserve.

I live in a city where the people ask you, "So, what do you do?" before they ask you your name or your Starbucks order. Your occupation is your identifier; your name is supplemental information. Your career becomes the defining characteristic of your identity. For better or worse, you are what you do. I imagine if we are too enmeshed in any one identity as the primary focus for who we are, it's hard to cope when and if that identity is disrupted.

I was blessed and cursed with parents who told me I could do anything I wanted, be anything I wanted. It provided me an incredible amount of support for whatever I was exploring and left the burden of the decision up to me. The only real clear guidelines were that I had to prioritize my education, and I had to accomplish something. Whatever I would choose to do was fine, but I *had* to choose.

The freedom to choose is equally liberating and confining, but it is far better than having no choice at all. Choice requires action, action breeds opportunity, and opportunity leads to building a life. The family examples of accomplishment were clear; doctorates or advanced degrees were the norm, expertise was a given, and careers of significance and stature standard practice. Often our expectations of ourselves can grow based more on the examples we are given than the directives provided. There was nothing wrong with the examples I was given. I am enormously proud of the accomplishments of my family, but it set the tone for what "you can do anything" meant.

I was never dissuaded from a life in the theater or music. I was never told, "That's nice and fun, but what are you going to do to make money? You can't make money at theater or music. What are you going to do for a real job?" As long as I was committed to it and doing something that illustrated that commitment, they were all in. I'm sure my parents worried. Maybe they felt like Carol and thought, "Why can't she just do something normal and financially stable?" But, if they did, they never said that to me, thankfully.

My kid is looking at a theater major. I mentioned that to a friend of mine the other day, and they said the same thing Carol did. As if automatically, it just came out of their mouth. This person knows of my kid's love of the theater, knows I have made a career based in no small part on my theater background, but still, their innate reaction was judgment. That's unfortunate.

* * *

I had a hard time figuring out where I fit in as a young person. It didn't always make sense to me. Much of my childhood was split between music and horses, building to a point where I had to choose between the two because doing both was too hard to manage. We moved from Indiana to Maryland after my freshman year of high school. After finding a place to feed my music habit at the Peabody Institute in Baltimore, we set about figuring out how to reengage with the horse stuff.

All the horse stuff in Indiana was a blast. I grew up riding at a small barn, learning from a small and serious woman. Most of the horse shows happened at the local fairgrounds, except for the time Sunny and I made it to the state fair in Indianapolis. I'd spend long weekends at the fairgrounds, compete in a couple events, hang out in the barns with my human and horse friends, eat amazingly terrible food—what more could you want? It was a family affair and a community event. Mom was with her friends wandering around the fair; Dad was schlepping the horse. I was not sure where my brother was; that is always a mystery—where my brother is. Your friends were there, your community was there, and even the people you didn't like so much but took a weird comfort in knowing were there.

When we moved to Maryland, we did everything we were supposed to as a family to continue my passion for riding. We had the right horse, the right trainer, the right barn, and the right horse shows. I tried it all on, and it didn't fit.

My father and I were at a horse show somewhere in Maryland with a rented roan beauty named Puff. Sunny was too old, too big, and lacked the breeding necessary for this new equine environment. We were sitting on the bed of Dad's truck at the end of a two-day horse show, waiting to leave. I had spent the previous evening staying overnight with a bunch of kids my own age, none of whom I knew. We stayed at one of the most beautiful barns I'd ever seen, sleeping above where our animals were resting before the next day's event. This was the last horse show my dad and I attended.

There was nothing wrong with any of those "right" things. But sitting on the back of Dad's pickup after that horse show, we both knew it wasn't for us. We didn't belong. There was nothing wrong with the new horse community; it just wasn't ours. Some activities transcend the communities they are attached to, and some are dependent on them. My love of horses (and specifically my love of Sunny) transcended the community it was attached to, but the activities surrounding it, the training and horse shows, did not. Without the community in Indiana, it just wasn't the same. At that point, my identity as an equestrian dissolved. I felt an incredible sense of guilt letting go of my life in the horse world. My parents had put in so much time and expense and commitment to it, as had I, but it didn't feel right anymore. To any of us.

* * *

We all move in and out of spaces, trying on identities and experiences to figure out who we are and where we fit. Some of what we discover lasts a lifetime, some only a little while. Researchers and advocates Micah Rajunov and Scott Duane, the editors of the book *Nonbinary: Memoirs of Gender and Identity*, write, "We all carry visible and invisible identities. Like gender, some of our identities are immediately evident to strangers, while others are misinterpreted, misconstrued, or hidden. Some identities elicit pride; others shame. Most of them are accompanied by an inherited or chosen community of others with similar stories, uniting us through common characteristics or experiences."

Wherever we land, however, and with whomever we identify, we understand we have to belong somewhere. To belong is to be safe and secure, to know with whom and where you fit. Without belonging, we are adrift and vulnerable. Evolutionarily, we need that belonging to survive. It has been baked into us from the beginning, like our fight-or-flight reflex and our need to eat chocolate after a bad day. Our identity and to which group we belong are fused together, like their own little Reese's peanut butter cup, two great tastes that taste great together. It is hard to think about one without the other.

* * *

It took me a while to figure out I was an entrepreneur. Once I did, second to being my kid's mom, it is the place I feel most like I belong. In one way or another, I always have been an entrepreneur, whether I understood it or not. Although I was doing the work of an entrepreneur, it wasn't a word I really vibed with. I didn't know what it meant. It seems so far away from my life with music or theater or horses or whatever else I was exploring. Entrepreneurship was the realm of men and start-up culture—dot coms and dudes. In my mind, creative and artsy people weren't entrepreneurs. It wasn't clear to me where I fit into the mix. My creative world seemed so far away from that life; no one I knew was an entrepreneur, and it wasn't an example of an accomplishment I was given.

Still today, more men are entrepreneurs. Although women, and Black women specifically, are the fastest-growing segment of entrepreneurs, both are still aggressively underfunded, as are all entrepreneurs of color, compared to their white male counterparts. Many transgender entrepreneurs, like other entrepreneurs from marginalized communities, come to the work because they don't feel welcome in the traditional workforce. Entrepreneurship is growing. The way we work is changing, and if we can equitably distribute the resources to support that growth to all who want to participate it will be all good. Unfortunately, there is still a lot of work to do in that area.

I started my first company at twenty-four, my second a nonprofit at twenty-five. I went on to produce theater in NYC for a decade before transitioning my entrepreneurial skills inside larger institutions. As I continued to use my skills to build things and convince people to pay me to do just that, I still didn't know what to call the work I was doing. I would create a program or a project that solved a specific problem for the institution. Upon completion, I would bounce to another opportunity to build something new. It was not unlike the work of producing a show. Each project would have a beginning, a middle, and an end, with specific metrics to determine its success. My work in the theater created a blueprint for how to approach each of these new projects— but I still didn't know how to identify the work I was doing. People would ask me, "So, what do you do?" and I wasn't quite sure how to answer them or how to come up with a clear answer for myself.

I now recognize I was an entrepreneur while running my own business, but if I am using the same skills while working for another institution, am I not an entrepreneur anymore? And now, as I am back working for myself, am I more of an entrepreneur now than I was then? My head hurts thinking about it, trying to fit what I do neatly into the word "entrepreneur," a word coined by French economist Jean-Baptiste Say back in the early 1800s. A word that has been redefined by many other economists and scholars over the years. A word that has proven its adaptability and therefore can either be or not be whatever I need it (or not) to be. I finally made the choice that it didn't matter whether I fit into Say's or anyone else's definition. It only mattered if naming myself an entrepreneur felt good for me.

How we choose to identify ourselves and name ourselves *should* feel good to us, not serve the purpose for others. We can change the rules, use the words we want, and redefine them to help communicate who we know we are. An entrepreneur and community builder friend of mine calls himself the Chief Dot Connector. He has multiple projects and businesses going on at the same time, serves as a community leader, and is always moving in and out of spaces doing the work that matters to him. But at the core, he serves as someone who connects art to opportunity, resources to community, and fellow entrepreneurs to their audience. He connects the dots. Taking artist and dot enthusiast Yayoi Kusama at her word, my friend recognizes that "with just one polka dot, nothing can be achieved."

* * *

Entrepreneurship is first a mindset and then a way of doing business. It requires creativity, good listening skills, a problem-solving approach, and the willingness to see the market gap that needs to be filled. It is about connecting those dots. Where that work happens, either in the NYC theater district or inside a government agency is less important to me than the fact that the work does happen. Maybe not intentionally, but I believe my parents' approach, leaving me be, to find my own way and solve my own problems, matched with my creative inclinations, led me easily to a life as an entrepreneur. But it was my theater training that sealed the deal.

My theater training taught me most of the essential skills necessary to be an entrepreneur: team building, creative problem-solving, navigating passionate constituents and building consensus, active listening, building something out of nothing, and so much more. Entrepreneurship requires you to understand business, in addition to thinking outside the box and questioning the status quo. My arts training was a perfect pathway to building those essential entrepreneurial skills and is the backbone of the career I have today.

I can only imagine that Carol may be hoping that the course of study her child chooses in college is the necessary step toward a job that can support her. But it's impossible to future-proof her life choices. The reality is there is no guarantee. There is data to suggest that the major you choose has a correlation to the income you make, but that data doesn't take into account all the multitude of factors that lead to a job you actually want to do, that supports the life you want to live. So, it's probably best to just chill out about it and not assume our college major, or whether we go to college at all, is the only answer to our future success.

All this being said, it's possible that Carol's frustration might be based on her fear that her child will be living in her basement forever, a fear many parents have. There is no way to know whether Carol's child will take her theater knowledge and turn it into an entrepreneurial career, have an active career as a working actor, be an amazing teacher, launch the next best product, or start a whole new path that has nothing to do with the arts. But with 76 percent of Generation Z describing themselves as responsible for driving their own career, I have a feeling she will take a proactive approach, make her own choices, and make the most out of all the skills she has.

DEAR DIARY, IT'S STILL NOT YOU, IT'S ME

"Mi querida Maria... Mary Ann is reasonably well organized for the week we'll be in Japan. Cathryn is, of course, concerned, but the truth is one can't really tell seventeen-year-old girls what to do. The boys are much more pliable at that age, but Mary Ann is of the independent-minded type, and there is no one to blame for that except us since we've pushed independence and self-sufficiency non-stop for seventeen years."

—MY DAD (FROM A LETTER SENT TO HIS SISTER, LUCIANA, IN 1989)

Dear Diary,

It has been a long time since we've connected, and I wanted to let you know I think of you often. I hope you found a home to provide you the love and attention you deserve. I have learned a lot in your absence. And although I still am not eager to rekindle our relationship, I have recently discovered the value of putting words on a page. You were right: writing has been a blessing. A tool to better understand myself. To explore what I know to be true, what I'm trying to figure out, and what I know nothing about. It brings order to the thoughts and feelings in a way I hadn't imagined it could. Words strung together are just as malleable as notes on the staff. They can create a vibe, build tension, and let out steam. Words can tame the chaos and let the wild horses run. I have learned how to write down my thoughts and feelings without you. It feels better without the pressure to fill your pages. It feels free. I didn't notice it until you were gone how oppressive your blank pages and silent presence were. I have learned that I don't need to sing other people's words and interpret other people's stories to express my feelings. And I don't need you to hold them for me. I have learned by reading the family letters and through my own writing that there is more value in reading to remember than I originally thought. I still want to experience and allow what fades to fade and what stays to stay. Not everything needs to be captured, but it feels less like a risk now, and it is who I am.

I AM WOMAN
AND I HAVE BEEN
KNOWN TO ROAR

———

Interviewer to Helen Reddy: "Do you really care what Australians think of Helen Reddy?"
Helen Reddy: "I care what Helen Reddy thinks of Helen Reddy. That's the most important thing."

I am sitting in an empty mezzanine of the Music Box Theater in New York City, watching one of my childhood heroes perform in the only Broadway show of her career. The orchestra seating below me is full, but if there are ten people scattered behind me, that would be a stretch.

I am in the front row of the mezzanine, the best vantage point to experience a musical. There is a misconception that the front of the orchestra section hosts the best seats in the house. I beg to differ. To really see a show, especially a musical, you need perspective. The front of the mezzanine, usually the lowest balcony in a traditional theater, will hang over roughly half or a third of the orchestra, which provides you a perfect distance from the stage. The real magic comes from your elevation, not your distance. What you see from the orchestra is driven by who is at the front of the stage; your fixed position in the audience establishes a myopic view of only the action right in front of you. That action can be compelling, but it is only one view of the story. From the front of the mezzanine, you can see the stage in all its glory. You get the central action the orchestra seat provides, but you also see who and what is behind and off to the side. You have perspective. That perspective is vital. All those surrounding elements are key to the action; they help you understand what the moment or the scene is actually about. If you are only looking at that one thing that exists in the center of your view, you miss the full point of the play. You miss the whole experience.

Most performative art forms require a team to tell the story. The world of theater is not a solo act, which is one of the brilliant and beautiful elements of the art form. There is a guiding vision for what the audience sees, a vision that has been crafted and manipulated to serve the story being told and inspire a reaction from the audience.

Tonight I couldn't give a shit about any of that. I don't see the scenery or lighting or hear the sound design or the orchestrations or see the costumes. All I know is Helen Reddy is singing to me. She could have been standing on the loading dock by the dumpster at night in her PJs, and I would be equally mesmerized.

I would like to claim that my admiration of Helen Reddy came from her status as a feminist icon. Her anthem, "I Am Woman," was released the year I was born, in 1972. It would be dazzling if I could say every little piece of my feminist leanings was tied to the serendipity of being born the year of the song's release. But the truth lies on the belly of an invisible green and purple dragon named Pete. I was five years old in 1977 when the movie *Pete's Dragon* was released, and Helen Reddy's Nora stood on the balcony of a lighthouse singing a different anthem, "Candle on the Water."

It is hard to determine how and why, but to this day, the sound of her voice triggers something deep inside me that I don't quite understand. Arguably. she had one of the most distinguishable voices of her generation. I'm sure that if I did my due diligence and dug down deep, I could determine a specific reason for the emotional reaction I have to hearing her voice—but I don't actually want to know. I don't really care. I just want to feel it. Some things just are, and they don't require a justification for them to be. So there I sit, alone in the front of the Music Box mezzanine, overwhelmed with emotion as Helen Reddy sings. To me.

* * *

I am woman.

I know I am a woman. I take it for granted. Although I know it to be true, I've never really thought about what it means. Not until my child started questioning their gender identity did it ever cross my mind that I had the option to question it as well.

I recognize the components of my gender that are based on society's expectations; they have been laid out on the table for me to absorb and follow. I certainly have experienced those expectations from others. I don't know a woman who hasn't. That explains what the outside world expects of me, but it doesn't help me understand what being a woman means to me. I watch my child move through the world and am a witness to their exploration. They are wildly in touch with both their personal experience of their gender as well as other people's expectations of them based on the aforementioned societal demands. I've had never really thought about the distinction between the two.

I imagine my lack of introspection about my own gender comes in part due to the fact that I never had to think about it. I could take it for granted. I am white, well educated, and identify with the gender I was assigned at birth. I grew up middle class, food and shelter secure, and I felt loved by parents who were present and provided for my needs. I am the beneficiary of my own ordinariness in those terms. I fit neatly into an acceptable category. What I am supposed to look like, do, earn, and say—and how and to whom I can say it—is certainly judged, but my presence is not. My presence is part of my privilege.

My child doesn't enjoy the same privilege I do. They have inherited their father and my complexion, are also well educated, middle class, and food and shelter secure. They feel loved by their parents, who are present and provide for their needs. They do not identify with the gender they were assigned at birth. That adjustment bumps them into a category that somehow triggers people to question my child's presence and other children like them, which is absurd. I wish it were our differences that drew us toward each other, not our sameness. I wish people would recognize some things just are and don't require a justification for them to be.

* * *

I am woman and…

When I was younger, I always wanted to hang out with the boys. Maybe it was due to my connection with my father or my desire to compete with my brother and be included by my older male cousin. When we visited the cousins' farm in the Pacific Northwest, the boys were always doing the fun stuff. They were riding ATVs and hypnotizing whole coups full of chickens (which is easier than you think)—they were making a mess and having adventures. I wanted to do that.

There is something about that traditional masculine energy that feels comfortable to me. If more masculine traits include toughness, ambition, and assertiveness, both the men and women in my family embodied these traits. If my femininity lies in my ability to be compassionate, empathetic, relational, or emotional, I resemble those elements as well, but so do the men in my family. I am a combination of all those things. Aren't we all a mix of these characteristics? I'm good with the broad identifier of *woman*, but as we get more specific with the labels, they start to frustrate me. If I am empathetic or relational or emotional, then I am feminine. If I am tough, ambitious, and assertive, then I am masculine. I'd rather just stick with the specifics and be empathetic, relational, emotional, tough, ambitious, assertive, and whatever else I am the day in question—and bypass the qualifiers feminine and masculine.

I don't like feeling like my gender is a scientific discovery that needs to be classified and labeled in terms of its taxonomy for people to understand who I am. I don't think there is a standard rubric for what makes a woman—and I'd prefer if we stopped trying to fit people into one. I have no claim on how others adopt or don't adopt the words women use to describe themselves. I agree with professor Stryker when she says, "Labeling others contrary to how they have labeled themselves is an ethically loaded act, but 'woman' remains a useful shorthand for the entanglement of femininity and social status regardless of biology—not as an identity, but as the name for an imagined community that honors the female, enacts the feminine and exceeds the limitations of a sexist society."

* * *

I have been known to roar.

"Lions are the only known cat species where individuals roar together—with even young cubs joining in with their mews. Prides often roar together to mark their territory." The pride comes together to make a low, guttural, resonant sound that can be heard up to five miles away. They plant their flag in the ground and let all within earshot know that they are here, here to stay. Lions use their voice, their roar, as a survival mechanism. It protects them and informs potential threats to back the fuck off—and they do it together.

I have wasted enough time watching cute cat videos, as has 80 percent of the rest of us—but have you ever watched lion cubs learning to roar? After you stop smiling and cooing, it's worth noticing what you don't see on those videos. You don't see momma or daddy lion telling their cubs to be seen but not heard, other pride mates calling them a bitch for roaring loudly, or their fellow cubs dismissing their roar outright for being not good enough. What you do see is that they are encouraged and empowered. The cub's ability to roar, and roar loudly, is essential to the survival of the pride.

Our voice is our most powerful resource. Some use their voice out of priority, others out of necessity—but too many don't use their voice at all. No matter the barriers that stand in the way of speaking your mind, and there are many, what is on your mind is meant to be spoken. For women and marginalized communities, there are layers of systemic and experiential subjugation that have a way of rendering one mute. The more you are talked over, your ideas ignored, your presence dismissed, your right to your body bartered—the more you are shown your voice doesn't matter—the louder you *must* roar. Your voice, our collective voices, are essential to the survival of the pride.

Maybe part of understanding how I feel about being a woman is knowing the woman I am doesn't need to be specifically defined. I can be woman, and I can roar. I can be wise. I can be born of pain and understand all I have gained. I can be strong and invincible. Because I can do anything. For I am a woman.

EPILOGUE: IT'S YOUR STORY TO TELL

———

"Who you are authentically is alright."

—LAVERNE COX

No matter what your story is, it matters. Everyone's story, our identities, are an amalgamation of all the experiences and interactions, connections, and beliefs we have had up to this point. They may be tied to your family, to your background, to your faith, or to your community, but you are the captain. You are the one who is strong, stands tall, and chooses where and how and to whom you anchor your ship. You also own the right to raise that anchor and move on however you choose.

You get to choose who you are and what you stand for. It will anger some and delight others. But your choice shouldn't be intended to elicit either of those responses. Your story is yours to understand. Your story is for you. It can be shared or not. Again, that is up to you.

But remember, your presence is powerful. Your story is essential, and the telling of that story, whether with a megaphone or one-on-one, has impacts beyond yourself. The one who tells the story owns the narrative. Time and again, narratives are constructed about people, about communities, and those people and communities are bypassed in the telling of that story. Historically, certain stories designed and told by the people who lived them have been erased. The distance between who designs the story and who tells the story needs to be removed. You have the power to impact that. You have more power than you know.

There is no ending to this story, to my story. This collection is only the beginning of an ongoing investigation, one I hope continues to keep me curious and engaged in better understanding myself. The labels Indiana, mother, woman, proud single parent, single, father's daughter, creative, entrepreneur, and curious are all part of the messy word cloud that is my identity today. I certainly don't have all the answers about who I am, but I know more than I did when I started this journey. I know the better I know myself, the easier it is to discover what I want. Our goals and desires are tied to who we know ourselves to be.

Our lives don't unfold like a novel. They are episodic and don't always have a clean narrative. They are a collection of essays. They are full of complicated situations and amazing experiences, tragic circumstances and loving interactions, heartbreak and redemption, and confusion and understanding. My life story is mine. Your life story is yours, and no one but you has the power to write it, to speak it, and to share it. However it comes out of you, let it. It's okay if it's messy. It's okay not to know. But it's not okay to not be curious. A complicated life, a messy life, is a full life, a life lived. And that life matters. That story matters and should only be told by you.

CITATIONS, NOTES,
AND COMMENTARY

———

Epigraph

Goodreads. "David Sedaris Quotes (Author of Me Talk Pretty One Day)." Accessed October 17, 2021. https://www.goodreads.com/author/quotes/2849.David_Sedaris.

Mother of a Daughter

InternetPoem.com. "A Servant to Servants Poem by Robert Frost." Accessed October 1, 2021. https://internetpoem.com/robert-frost/a-servant-to-servant-poem/.

Obama, Michelle. *Becoming*. London: Penguin Books, 2018.

It's Not Your Story to Tell

Health Foundations. "A Brief (and Fascinating) History of Breastfeeding and Its Alternatives." Accessed September 11, 2021. https://www.health-foundations.com/blog/2015/01/05/a-brief-and-fascinating-history-of-breastfeeding-and-its-alternatives.

Joan Didion. "We tell ourselves stories to live." Accessed October 1, 2021. https://www.thejoandidion.com/didion-quotes-1/2016/3/31/we-tell-ourselves-stories-in-order-to-live.

Where Are You from?

Florida, Richard. "The Great Mobility Divide." *Bloomberg*. October 12, 2017. https://www.bloomberg.com/news/articles/2017-10-12/ america-is-divided-between-the-mobile-and-the-stuck.

Olmstead, Grace. Uprooted Recovering the Legacy of the Places We've Left Behind. New York: Sentinel, 2021.

The Sound of Silence

Doyle, Arthur Conan. "The Man With the Twisted Lip" from *The Adventures of Sherlock Holmes*. Mineola: Dover, 2010.

Hartemann, Gabby Omoni. "Stop Erasing Transgender Stories From History." Sapiens. March 31, 2021. https://www.sapiens.org/ archaeology/transgender-people-exist-in-history/.

Lowry, Lois. *The Giver*. Boston: Houghton Mifflin Harcourt, 2018.

Ask and You Shall Receive

National Geographic Society. "Interview With Sylvia Earle, Ocean-ographer." Accessed August 30, 2021. https://kids.nationalgeographic.com/pages/article/interview-with-sylvia-earle.

Grant, Adam M. Think Again: The Power of Knowing What You Don't Know. New York City: Viking Books, 2021.

My Father's Daughter

Campbell, Joseph. *Myths to Live By*. New York: Penguin/Arkana, 1993.

Stets, Jan E. and Peter J Burke. "Identity Theory and Social Identity Theory." Social Psychology Quarterly. Volume 63, Number 3 (2000): pp. 224-237. https://doi.org/10.2307/2695870.

In Praise of Crying: An Instagram Caption

Brown, Brené. "'The Power of Vulnerability" Filmed June 2010. TEDx-
    Houston, 20:03. https://www.ted.com/talks/brene_brown_
    the_power_of_vulnerability?language=en.

I'd Rather Be the Verb Than a Noun

Delistraty, Cody C. "Can Creativity Be Learned?" *The Atlantic*. July
    16, 2014. https://www.theatlantic.com/health/archive/2014/07/
    can-creativity-be-learned/372605/.
Radner, Gilda. *It's Always Something*. Sydney: Simon and Schuster,
    1989.

Can I Please Get a Decent Bra with My Fireball Shot?

Barry, Dave. *Dave Barry Is from Mars and Venus*. New York: Bal-
    lantine Books, 1998.
World Population Review. "Seward, Alaska Population 2021."
    Accessed September 10, 2021. https://worldpopulationreview.com/
    us-cities/seward-ak-population.

How ~~Not~~ to Parent a Queer Child

Glennon, I love a good quote bank, and Brainy Quote certainly
    holds the best cache or has the strongest SEO game of the
    bunch. Was hoping to find the original source material for
    this one.
BrainyQuotes "Glennon Doyle Melton Quotes." Accessed October
    10, 2021. https://www.brainyquote.com/quotes/glennon_doyle_
    melton_899029.
Fetters, Ashley. "The Many Faces of the 'Wine Mom'" *The
    Atlantic*, May 23, 2020. https://www.theatlantic.com/family/
    archive/2020/05/wine-moms-explained/612001/.
PFLAG (Parents, Families, and Friends of Lesbians and Gays)
    defines LGBTQ+ the following way: "LGBTQ+: An acronym

that collectively refers to individuals who are lesbian, gay, bisexual, transgender, or queer, sometimes stated as LGBT (lesbian, gay, bisexual, and transgender) or, historically, GLBT (gay, lesbian, bisexual, and transgender). The addition of the Q for queer is a more recently preferred version of the acronym as cultural opinions of the term queer focus increasingly on its positive, reclaimed definition (see *Queer*). The Q can also stand for questioning, referring to those who are still exploring their own sexuality and/or gender. The "+" represents those who are part of the community, but for whom LGBTQ does not accurately capture or reflect their identity."

PFLAG. "PLAG National Glossary of Terms." Accessed July 15, 2021. https://pflag.org/glossary.

One Hundred Heart Pillows

Wilde, Oscar. *An Ideal Husband*. Mineola (New York): Dover Publications, 2015.

You Bring Them

St. Vincent Millay, Edna. *Letters of Edna St. Vincent Millay*. Edited by Allan Ross MacDougall. New York: Grosset & Dunlap, 1952.

Woolf, Virginia. *The Waves*. New York, NY: Harvest Books, 1978.

This Single Parent Is Far from Broken

Kanter, Rosabeth Moss. "Ten Reasons People Resist Change." Accessed October 28, 2019. https://hbr.org/2012/09/ten-reasons-people-resist-chang.

Merriam-Webster. "Breakdown." Accessed October 12, 2021. https://www.merriam-webster.com/dictionary/breakdown.

Sylvester, Brad. "Fact Check: Did Ernest Hemingway Say, 'We Are All Broken—That's How the Light Gets in'?" Accessed

October 28, 2019. https://checkyourfact.com/2019/10/28/fact-
check-ernest-hemingway-quote-all-broken-light/.

Yoko Ono (@yokoono). "If the rules are not broken, we will be."
Twitter, April 10, 2017. https://twitter.com/yokoono/status/
851442142924988416?lang=en.

When an Omani Man Asks You to Go Back to His Camel Farm, He Actually Wants You to Meet His Camels

Adichie, Chimamanda Ngozi. "The Danger of a Single Story."
Filmed July 2009. TEDGlobal video, 18:33. https://www.ted.com/
talks/chimamanda_ngozi_adichie_the_danger_of_a_single_
story?language=en.

McBee, Thomas Page. *Amateur: A True Story about What Makes
a Man*. Edinburgh: Canongate, 2019.

Why Can't I Have a Lesbian Lover as Attentive as the Woman in 6B?

Brontë Charlotte. *The Letters of Charlotte Brontë: With a Selection
of Letters by Family and Friends*. Edited by Margaret Smith.
Vol. III. Oxford: Oxford University Press, 2004.

Brown, Anna. "Nearly Half of U.S. Adults Say Dating Has Gotten
Harder for Most People in the Last 10 Years." Pew Research
Center, October 2, 2020. https://www.pewresearch.org/social-
trends/2020/08/20/nearly-half-of-u-s-adults-say-dating-has-
gotten-harder-for-most-people-in-the-last-10-years/.

Brown, Patrick T. "U.S. Marriage Rates Hit New Recorded Low."
United States Joint Economic Committee, April 29, 2020.
https://www.jec.senate.gov/public/index.cfm/republicans/
2020/4/marriage-rate-blog-test.

Goleman, Daniel. "Erikson, in His Own Old Age, Expands His
View of Life." *New York Times*. Accessed October 3, 2021.

https://archive.nytimes.com/www.nytimes.com/books/
99/08/22/specials/erikson-old.html.

Wolpert, Stuart. "UCLA neuroscientist's book explains why social
connection is as important as food and shelter" *UCLA News-
room,* October 10, 2013. https://newsroom.ucla.edu/releases/
we-are-hard-wired-to-be-social-248746.

You Look Good for Your Age

Los Angeles Times. "Rose Kennedy, 104, Dies; Matriarch of a
Dynasty." Accessed October 16, 2021. https://www.latimes.com/
la-me-ted-kennedy-timeline-rose-kennedy-dies-story.html.

Oh Crap, I Just Should All Over Myself

Lieberman, Matthew D. *Social: Why Our Brains Are Wired to Connect.* Oxford: Oxford University Press, 2013.

Menotti, Gian Carlo, Frances Frost, and Roger Duvoisin. *Gian-
Carlo Menotti's Amahl and The Night Visitors.* London: Andrew
Dakers Ltd., 1953.

Wagner, Jane. *The Search for Signs of Intelligent Life in the Universe.*
New York: Harper & Row, 1986. This quote was written by Jane
Wagner for Lily Tomlin's 1977 one-woman show *The Search for
Signs of Intelligent Life in the Universe,* which was later turned
into a movie in 1991.

What Is a Real Job, Anyway?

Gelber, Mack. "Here's What You Need to Know About Gen
Z." Accessed October 13, 2021. https://www.monster.com/
career-advice/article/gen-z-boss-0816.

GEM Global Entrepreneurship Monitor."2019 Women's Entrepreneurship Report." November 18m 2019.
https://www.gemconsortium.org/report/gem-20182019-womens-
entrepreneurship-report. GEM is a fantastic resource with

research reports on the state of entrepreneurship going back
to 1999. The dismal state funding for nonwhite male entrepreneurs is well documented from a variety of sources.

Hepner, Guy. "Into the World of Yayoi Kusama: Guy Hepner NYC."
Accessed May 28, 2021. https://www.guyhepner.com/into-the-
world-of-kusama/.

This quote is widely attributed to Coco Chanel. I found this page
that gives a little background on the quote.

Quote Investigator. "In Order to Be Irreplaceable One Must Always
Be Different." Quote Investigator, June 11, 2019.
https://quoteinvestigator.com/2019/06/11/irreplaceable/.

Rajunov, Micah, and A. Scott Duane. *Nonbinary: Memoirs of Gender and Identity.* New York: Columbia University Press, 2019.

I Am a Woman and I Have Been Known to Roar

60 Minutes Australia. "Iconic feminist Helen Reddy's must-see
interview." September 2, 2020. 11:21.
https://youtu.be/38TbjQtxlWw.

Reddy, Hellen. "I Am Woman." Accessed September 25, 2021.
https://genius.com/Helen-reddy-i-am-woman-lyrics.

Stryker, Susan. "What Does It Mean to Be a Woman? It's Complicated." Accessed March 5, 2020. https://time.com/5795626/
what-womanhood-means/.

University of Utah. "Born to roar: Lions' and tigers' fearsome roars
are due to their unusual vocal cords." Accessed October 14, 2021.
www.sciencedaily.com/releases/2011/11/111102190012.htm.

Epilogue: It's Your Story to Tell

Nichols, James. "Laverne Cox Shares Her Journey To Living
Authentically As A Trans Woman." HuffPost, February 2, 2016.
https://www.huffpost.com/entry/laverne-cox-it-got-better_
n_5511230.

ACKNOWLEDGMENTS

Thank you to my kid for giving me the gift of their strength, wisdom, and spirit. You are the joy of my life. And thank you for giving me the green light to do this in the first place. Without that, this book would never have seen the light of day. Thank you to my ex-husband for giving me the gift of my child. You are an amazing dad.

Thank you to my parents for giving of their time, attention, love, support, and patience, along with passing along their DNA. Without any of those things, I wouldn't be here today. Also, thank you both for cultivating your moderate hoarding tendencies and keeping all the family stuff, especially all those letters. Thank you to my brother for not kicking the shit out of me when I slapped him and for shoving that one guy in the locker when he was an ass to me. You are brilliant, and I feel better knowing you are behind the scenes changing the world.

Thank you to the ladies I have met through the Cru. You guys have been such a welcome support during an incredibly vulnerable time. Rashaan, Celena, Rachel, Shamon, Tammi, Tonya, Bernadette, many others, and our fearless leader of the Writers Group, Dr. Marsie—thank you all!

Thank you to the many people with whom I've had conversations about the book, those who have shared with me their identity stories, and those whose insights have helped shape my thinking. The gift of your time and insight were invaluable. The ability to talk ideas out and work them through made it easier to not only understand myself but also how to bring it to the page.

Thank you to the Creators Institute and New Degree Press team, especially Erik Koester, Katie Sigler, and Whitney McGruder. You all were instrumental in getting me to this point. And thank you to the amazing fellow authors and author coaches I've connected with through this process. It is truly a community with a team ready and able and excited to help when needed.

Thank you to these wonderful people who got in the game a little early and grabbed a copy of the book during the presale. Your contributions, encouragement, feedback, DMs, heart emojis have made this book possible! Ester Ackerman, Quentin Shawn Addison, Shamon Allen, Jennifer Asher, Karen Baker, Joanna Ball, Melanie Baskurt, Kate Becker, Joshua Belhumeur, Gabriel 'Asheru' Benn, Ashlee Berghoff, Nabeeh Bilal, Jenny Bilfield, Sue Ellen Bisgaard, Michael Bracy, Julianne Brienza, Christine Brooks-Cropper, Austin Brower, Bryant Brown, Kayona Ebony Brown, Lemond Brown, Kathryn Bugg, Rev. Sandra Butler-Truesdale, Will Carroll, Craig Cassey, Lauren Cattaneo, Anna Celenza, Melanie

Charleton, Randy Chertkow, Donna Cooper, Karen Corso, Debbie Curtis, Kate DeRaedt, Mary DeRaedt, Sarah DeRaedt Banks, Kyrisha Deschamps, Brandon Dubé, Jacoby DuBose, Mia DuVall, Mentwab Easwaran, Robert Ellis, Ella Epshteyn, Harley Erdman, Laura Fallon, Kassia Finkler, Dana Flor, Dawn Fong, Heather Frank, Justin Franks, Erin Frisby, Sharon Fross, Emma Fatemeh Amiri-Ghaemmaghamy, Michael Gargano, Angie M. Gates, Sam Gerard, Danielle Glosser, Hannah Grannemann, Celena Green, Julian Harris, Michael Holstein, Philippa Hughes, Malachai Johns, Bryant Johnson, Dare Johnson, Dwight Jones, Michelle Jones, Munch Joseph, Kelly King, Talya Kingston, Joe Kirgues, Heather Klinefelter, Eric Koester, Lance Kramer, Tim Krepp, Ron Lamlech, Adam Levin, Rita Lewis, Geoff Livingston, Rod Loges, Cathryn Lombardi, John L. Lombardi, John V. Lombardi, Shannon Lombardi, Kristen Lovano, Tammi Martin, Abby Maslin, Brandon McEachern, Kate Merehand, Danielle Mouledoux, Amit Nerurkar, Bridget Nistico, Kristina Noell, Greg Noonan, Gbenga Ogunjimi, S. Lovey Parker, Rick Parnell, Rashaan Peek, Lee Levingston Perine, Thomasina Perkins-Washington, Amber Philpott, Kim Philpott, Sharon Philpott, Adrienne Picciotto, Don Pitts, Cam Poles, Will Porter, Kathy Pugh, Jennifer Queen, Beth Rashleigh, Dana Ray, Chelsea Ritter-Soronen, Steven A. Rodreiguez, Michelle Rogers, Christine Ruksenas-Burton, Molly Ruland, Jeffery Scott, Matt Scott, Charlena Seymour, Bernadette Sheridan, Ramael Slater, Tiffany Thacker, Ken R. Thompson, Jeffery Tribble Jr., Nancy Urbschat, Elle VanDyne, Tonya Warren, Ray Williams, Jordann Wine, Catherine Wood, Indya Wright, Doug Yeuell, Nick Yowarski, and Fran G. Zarubrick.